*Relations and Revelations*

David Herbert

# Relations and Revelations
## Advice to Jemima

PETER OWEN · LONDON

PETER OWEN PUBLISHERS
73 Kenway Road London SW5 ORE
Peter Owen books are distributed in the USA by
Dufour Editions Inc. Chester Springs PA 19425–0449

First published in Great Britain 1992
© David Herbert 1992

A catalogue record for this book is available
from the British Library

ISBN 0–7206–0874–0

Printed in Great Britain by Billings of Worcester

I hope that this book will not appear to the reader pretentious or conceited, for it was written partly that it might perhaps be of help to the young in this violent and unpredictable world. I am grateful to Nicholas Shakespeare for suggesting the book and for persuading me to write it.

The Book of Life begins with a man and a woman in a garden. It ends with Revelations.

*Oscar Wilde*

# Illustrations

*The endpapers are based on a photograph of part of the author's garden in Tangier*

# Foreword

In Morocco the man in the street is not celebrated for his leniency in judging the behaviour of Europeans; on the contrary he holds a dim view of everything Nazarene. If in a specific instance this opinion alters to a more favourable one, as it can do, the change is a result of minute observation. The Moroccan has watched the European carefully over a period of time, and through personal experience has learned that this particular foreigner, although an unbeliever, has an ethical code, and moreover, actually observes it. The obsessive scrutiny of the long-term resident is as conclusive a test as acid for gold. A Moroccan peasant's assessment of the basic character of a European whom he knows well can be taken as conclusive.

For the past four decades David Herbert has lived in Djamaa el Mokra, a village on the side of the mountain just west of Tangier. There he has made his exquisite house, a nest hidden by the plant-life around it. The original inhabitants of Djamaa el Mokra will tell you that he is a 'good' man because he treats them as people. That is, he cares about what happens to them and their families, and is generous in his dealings with them.

The word *stamina* comes to mind. David does nothing half-heartedly. His reserves of energy are phenomenal. In residence, he will have thirty people to lunch and sixteen to dinner. He moves around almost as much as the long-haired members of the transient generation; you may find him walking on the ramparts at Essaouira, or watching the sacred fish in the gorge at Tinerhir. But his physical endurance is merely a coefficient of a more basic vitality, which I suspect comes of his being sure of who he is. If you really know exactly who you are, you will generally know just

9

what to do. (I don't mean knowing you are the son of an earl, although clearly that is a help in removing doubts.) I have never seen David at a loss as to how to proceed.

He is wonderfully hard to depress. Sometimes it has seemed that he took a perverse pleasure in insisting upon the purely hypothetical advantages of an intolerable situation. The optimism is not assumed, however, and often his expectations, sanguine beyond all reason, prove to have been justified.

Then there is his devouring social curiosity. He wants to know every kind of person there is, and in his house one is likely to meet just about that. All he asks is that each one be himself, that no one attempt to appear something else. If even the thinnest smoke-screen of pretence is spread, he will be sure to detect it, and then, sooner or later, you will hear the expression that denotes the ultimate in David's lexicon of disapproval: *second-rate*.

This visceral inquisitiveness transcends the concept of social hierarchy; for him who has it each person is an entity, potentially of the same interest and importance as the next. The Moroccans appreciate this virtue in a Nazarene probably more than any other, and one can be certain that it was the decisive factor in weighing the local scales in David Herbert's favour.

*Paul Bowles*

# 1

The following pages, or some of them, are a light-hearted attempt at being a guide to the teenager.

When you first grow up you will probably feel self-conscious. If you do, remember that it is a form of vanity. For instance, you walk into a room or a restaurant and you imagine everyone is looking at you, when in reality they have not even noticed your arrival. I was self-conscious when I first grew up. It is a thing of youth and gradually you realize how stupid you have been and your self-consciousness fades away.

Shyness is a different matter, and for a girl usually stems from some physical defect – too big a nose, fat legs, eyes too close together or being nearly blind without wearing pebble glasses. In order to get over these unfortunate defects it is difficult but not impossible if you make yourself into what is called 'a character' – dress outrageously, wear enormous tinted glasses with brightly coloured frames, grow a fringe, use a lot of make-up and put on as much costume jewellery as you can muster.

My cousin Lady Ursula Talbot would have been a beauty but for her nose, which was so big that it seemed to enter a room long before the rest of her. Because of this defect she was painfully shy, rarely spoke and was a wallflower at every débutante dance. Eventually she could bear it no longer and, unbeknown to her parents, had it chopped off and a little *retroussé* nose took its place. After this operation she never looked back. She had three husbands and between the second and third lived with a well-known English writer for many years. Sadly she was killed in a private plane, piloted by her third husband, over the Scilly Isles.

Another cousin of mine was Dorothy Paget, daughter of Lord Queenborough. She was remarkably plain and what made it worse she had a beautiful sister, Olive, Lady Baillie, of Leeds Castle. Poor Dorothy had skin like a ploughed field, an under-hung lower lip, mousy, rather thin hair and became enormously fat. Her saving grace was that she was destined to become very rich. When she came of age she inherited a vast fortune, which made her independent. She was able to lead the eccentric life she chose, by turning night into day. Buying racehorses was her one passion, but she was seldom seen on the racecourse, except if one of her horses was running in a particularly important race. Otherwise, she relied on the wireless, as it was then called, for the results of her racing activities. She was surrounded by ruthless sycophants who, for what they could get out of her, also turned their nights into days. What they didn't know was that she was fully aware of their goings-on but put up with them because it gave her a sense of power which, in a way, compensated for her inferiority complex. Her money was in trust, so they inherited nothing. Dorothy never married and to my knowledge had no lovers, male or female. She died when she was still quite a young woman.

If you grow up to be a classic beauty, beware. A lot of men shy away from these kinds of women out of a kind of reverence, for they usually lack sex appeal because they are more interested in guarding their beauty than giving it away to lovers.

Look out for anyone who says 'Thank God I've got a sense of humour', for it invariably means he or she has none. Another cousin of mine, Gwendolin Wilkinson, was one of these people. She was immensely tall and very beautiful, but dressed so badly and was so bossy and pleased with herself that she remained a spinster till she died in her eightieth year. Later in life she formed an attachment with a nurse at the hospital where she was working. My mother was chairman and was asked by the matron if she would convey to her niece Miss Wilkinson that it was not acceptable for her to enter another nurse's bed, however innocent the reason. An unpleasant task for my mother. Anyway, they both gave notice and set up a crèche for illegitimate children, all black, who had been born during the 1939–45 war when American troops were stationed in the neighbourhood. The crèche was situated in a lovely house called Clouds, formerly the home of the Wyndham family. The two ladies ran it for several years and then retired to a house in the village. Gwendolin is dead. Ada is still living and the house is named Gwenada!

Try hard not to be jealous. Nothing finishes a marriage or a love affair so quickly, as no one likes to be adored to that extent. In the end it becomes a kind of illness. Your imagination runs away with you and, unconsciously, you invent things to be jealous about. Hence your loved one is driven mad defending himself. 'But darling, I did lunch at the club yesterday'; 'It was for business reasons that I went to Glasgow last week'; and so on until it comes to the point where he throws up his hands and says: 'To hell with you, it seems I can't do anything right. You seem to think I lead a double life and everything I say is a pack of lies.' This sort of outburst is followed by tears and miserable scenes. Perhaps such a relationship may be patched up once or twice, but in the end the man just walks out.

He can stand it no more.

If as a child you are born of a rich family and later, when you grow up, you realize that your parents have lost everything in some financial crash or other, what's to be done? Have courage and think of the future as a new adventure. Try and forget what you were brought up to believe your life, as an adult, would be. Run away from home if necessary and find a job, *any* job. Be a barmaid, join a theatrical group as a chorus girl and forget the luxuries to which you have been accustomed. I did exactly that myself. I was cut off by my family and went to Berlin, where I became Otto Khan's secretary for a few weeks. I was sacked and then I sang in a night-club and during the day gave English lessons to German actors and actresses. I saved enough to sail on a slow boat to the United States, where I found work in an antique shop belonging to John and Dorothy Hamilton. Suddenly I remembered I used to draw, and started doing portraits of society ladies and famous actresses. I have never regretted my young life and was eventually welcomed home like the Prodigal Son!

Try not to be possessive of people. It is the cause of many broken relationships. If you have a missionary side to your character, of which you are hardly conscious, subjugate it if you can, because you can't change anyone – why should you think you are better than they? You married them or loved them probably for the very same faults that you are now trying to remedy. It isn't worth it, and if you think clearly about it, you will realize it is nothing but a form of conceit. I certainly had that streak in the past by trying to stop someone from drinking to excess. In the end he got fed up with my watering the vodka, hiding the whisky and so forth. It was sheer stupidity on my part, as he didn't want to stop drinking. So it ended by his going to live in Spain where, sadly, he drank himself to death. My only excuse, if I am to be excused, is that he was a brilliant man and the finest researcher that *Fortune* magazine ever employed. His name was James Caltery.

If you grow up with lesbian tendencies, it may well be a hangover from your having had a crush on the headmistress of your late school. This is a very common occurrence. It is frequently a case of growing pains. In boys' schools, many older boys fall in love with younger ones, as they did in my days at Eton. But that didn't necessarily mean that they were 'gay'. Most of them grew up to be perfectly normal. They married, had children and in some cases became famous as admirals, generals, ambassadors or governors of our once far-flung Empire. Certainly some grew up to be homosexual, but I am sure they were born that way and not made so by schoolboy love affairs.

However, I know cases of men and women who have led perfectly normal lives until a certain age and then quite suddenly discover that they prefer their own sex. This I think is more prevalent among women, who perhaps have not had a very happy married life and have reached the age when they are no longer attractive to men, so they find consolation in a form of *amitié amoureuse* with a partner of their own age and sex. If you are truly homosexual or lesbian, it is useless to fight against it. The thing to remember, I think, is not to embarrass people by flaunting your abnormality (if that is the correct word). Don't dress like a man and crop your hair if you are a woman, and don't make up your face and dye your hair if you are a man. If you do, some people will laugh at you. A good instance of this was Miss Radclyffe Hall and Una, Lady Trowbridge, as when they arrived at the opening of a new play (they always arrived late). The audience would rise and stare at them, suppressing giggles as best they could. Tallulah Bankhead once said: 'But darling, you must pity the poor lesbian who cannot whistle at her work!'

I remember once having dinner with Diana Cooper, Enid Bagnold the writer and her husband Sir Roderick Jones, a pompous little man and head of Reuters. The conversation turned to this subject and Diana said: 'I do think it's unfair that men are put in prison for being homosexual and lesbians get off scot-free. Why?' Enid piped up: 'Diana darling, be your age. No penetration, of course!' Sir Roderick exploded and left the table.

Arthur Macree, one of the wittiest men I have ever known, wrote sketches and lyrics for musical comedies and revues. One day Terry Rattigan, who had a new boy-friend who looked years younger than Terry, asked Arthur what he thought people would think if he took the young man to supper at the Ivy, where all the theatrical folk gathered after the shows ended. Arthur replied: 'I expect they would think you are a ventriloquist.'

Relationships between homosexual men, who are mostly promiscuous, rarely last very long, whereas lesbians are faithful to each other till 'death do us part'. I have no idea of the reason for this except that the sexual behaviour of the male is much more publicized than that of the female. I can only think that it is because there are many fewer 'gay' women than 'gay' men. There are thousands of bars and clubs all over the world for this type of man, but very few for women. In Holland, for instance, two men can get happily married and have their marriage approved of by the parents. This doesn't necessarily mean that fidelity continues for ever, for after a year or so they go their own ways yet remain friends, very much like couples in some normal marriages. The truth is that the average man is born to be 'unfaithful' while the woman is not. Certainly in southern countries the man seldom takes his wife out to bars or public places. Wives are left at home to manage the house and look after the children. I don't mean the 'upper classes' but the so-called 'people'. In northern countries couples go out together a great deal and get a baby-sitter, preferably a neighbour, to look after the kiddies.

I consider meanness to be one of the deadliest sins. Think of yourself grown up and discovering that a few of your friends are mean. It will make you feel uncomfortable and embarrassed for them. If, for instance, you have a girls' lunch in a restaurant and, when the bill comes, the mean one gets up and goes to the lavatory and stays there long enough, eventually out of embarrassment you will find yourself paying for her share as well as your own. Little by little the wretched girl will be dropped from your circle. There is no cure for this defect. The same thing applies to men. Certainly no girl will stay in love with a mean man, so most of them grow into friendless, crusty old bachelors.

There are different forms of meanness. I have known people of both sexes who are generous in big things but would die rather than put their hands in their bags or their pockets to give a tip or pay for a taxi. My cousin Lady Juliet Duff was like that. There was never quite enough food to go round at her weekend parties. Duff Cooper used to slink up to the 'Big House', as Wilton was called, and ask my mother for a biscuit because he was hungry! This was easy, as Juliet lived in the

Lord and Lady Herbert, the author's mother and father,
*c.* 1903

Dower House, just outside the Park gates. In other ways she was a generous woman and gave large sums of money to the ballet and many theatrical ventures which were in need of funds.

Juliet's son Michael, witty and eccentric, was the same. Everyone loved him. Staying at Vaynol, his home in North Wales, one enjoyed the height of luxury with masses of food and drink, but to get him to pay for a meal in a restaurant was like trying to extract blood from a stone. I remember arriving at 'the Pyramid' in Vienne, Isère, the most famous of all French restaurants at that period. Here we met up with Cyril Connolly and Christopher Sykes, two great gourmets; they were already studying the menu and smacking their lips in anticipation. When the head waiter asked Michael what he would like, he replied: 'Two sardines out of a tin, please.' The head waiter nearly had apoplexy and we almost sank under the table with embarrassment and laughter. This kind of meanness is perhaps pardonable. It is a question of a person not being able to part with cash, whereas writing cheques is all right , which perhaps at the time they don't count as actual money!

Juliet had a passion for a young man named Simon Carnes. In the war, when he joined the Merchant Navy, he changed his name to Simon Fleet. She gave him endless presents, including a house at Rye, where he could work undisturbed on a play he was writing. It was a happy relationship until Simon, who was very good-looking, said one evening after dinner: 'Well, how about it, old girl?' Juliet screamed: 'How dare you suggest such a thing! All I want in my bed is a book. Leave the house at once.' Simon walked, in the pitch-dark, through the woods to my house in the Park where he woke me up by banging loudly on my front door. 'What's happened, Simon?' I asked. He told me. Next morning, in fear and trembling, I went over to Juliet's house and begged her to forgive him. 'He really adores you, darling. It was just bad judgement on his part. He felt, in some way, the only thing he could give in return for your kindness was himself. After all, he is very good-looking and most unattached ladies would jump at the idea.' It worked; and they lived happily together for many years. Juliet died in her late seventies. Simon never got over her death and a year later he broke his neck by falling down the stairs in a little mews house in London which she had given him.

If you are born with an artistic temperament but, sadly, possess no actual talent either for acting, writing, painting or sculpting, what do you do? Perhaps the only way to use your artistic temperament is to be permanently on-stage yourself. Use your temperament to become a good talker. This can be achieved by mixing with the sort of people you would like to resemble, and by telling amusing anecdotes and quoting sayings of famous people in a flamboyant manner. Even if you don't know such people well, few will take the trouble to check up whether you were actually there when these incidents or conversations purportedly occurred. If you speak with enough verve, you will get away with it. Invent or exaggerate a little if you think this will help capture your audience. In this way you can at least feel you are contributing something to compensate for your lack of talent. My cousin Michael was an expert at this. He would keep people in fits of laughter with his stories and adventures. He had a stammer which he cultivated and would use at exactly the right moment, usually just before he delivered the punch line. Beatrice Guinness was another. I remember Osbert Sitwell coming up to us in the Ritz bar in London and saying: 'Good morning, Beatrice, my dear. I saw a friend of yours yesterday who. . . .' He got no further as Beatrice said: 'Impossible, Osbert. I have no friends.'

Princesse Edmond de Polignac, born Winnaretta Singer, was a well-known lesbian. Winnie lived in Paris or Venice when not on her yacht. She was adept at putting people in their place, but once, when a certain gentleman was very rude to her, she failed. Winnie turned on him and said: 'If you are the gentleman you are supposed to be, you will apologize and leave my house.' He replied: 'If you are the gentleman you pretend to be, I will challenge you to a duel.'

Lady Cholmondeley, Sybil to her friends, was a fascinating character. The last time I saw her she was very old and living in her beautiful house Houghton, in Norfolk. After lunch a rather pushy young man of around thirty arrived from the National Trust. Sybil was polite but resented this uninvited intrusion. On leaving, the young man said: 'I do hope I shall see you again.' Sybil replied: 'You might, young man. You look perfectly healthy to me.' A friend of mine and hers, Cecil Stuart, asked Sybil one day whether she should cut down a silver birch in her garden. Sybil replied: 'I shouldn't, if I were you. After all, the poor thing is naked all winter and only has a few spangles in the summer.'

I have known talented people who, because of their birth or position in life, have been unable to concentrate properly on their particular talent. A good example of this was Princess Marina, the late Duchess of Kent, who was an extremely good portraitist in watercolour. Some of her drawings, such as those of Lord Drogheda and of her daughter Princess Alexandra, are first rate. She didn't have the time to fulfil this talent, owing to her public work. For that reason she never collected enough of her drawings to have an exhibition. Not that I feel she would have, owing to her modesty. She was a good, kind, gentle person, a little shy and a truly loyal friend. Added to this she was full of humour and had a great sense of fun. I was devoted to her and valued her friendship enormously. The death of her beloved husband, the Duke, who was killed on active service in an air crash in Scotland on his way to Iceland, was a shattering blow. Prince Michael was a baby when this happened. My sister-in-law, Mary Pembroke, was the Duchess's lady-in-waiting and had the terrible task of breaking the sad news to her. Mary tells me how wonderful she was, not thinking of herself but of the others in the Sunderland flying-boat. She asked Mary to find out the names and telephone numbers of the wives of those who had been on board. She rang up each person and said: 'I am afraid I have to give you sad news – we are both widows.' Not until she had done this did she break down and collapse in shattering misery. Her sense of duty came first.

Lord Berners was another example of unfulfilled talent because he had too many: he painted, he wrote, he composed. But because he was a rich man, nothing he did was really first-rate. He was wildly clever and always amusing but remained a dilettante, having no need to make money. He was also a true eccentric and in his will he stipulated that he was to be stuffed and hung in a glass case over the drawing-room mantle-piece in his Berkshire house, Faringdon.

This reminds me that when the late Lord Faringdon (no relation of Lord Berners), a bachelor when he succeeded his father, rose to make his maiden speech in the House of Lords, instead of addressing his fellow-peers with the traditional 'My Lords', he began: 'My Dears'.

I do hope you don't grow up to be a snob. It is so old-fashioned: nobody cares any more where you come from as long as you are yourself. Marrying 'beneath' one, as it used to be called, doesn't exist any more. When I was young, nobody of the 'upper classes' would think of entertaining let alone marrying a hair-dresser, a dentist, a masseur or a beauty specialist. Doctors, on the other hand, were difficult; they were asked, perhaps once a year, to tea. Even clergymen, unless they came from a good family, were also on the 'asked to tea' list. At Wilton we had a wonderful vicar, Guy Campbell, a member of the Cawdor clan. He married Lord Valentia's daughter and remained with us for many years, living in the lovely Queen Anne rectory. He was also private chaplain to my family and took prayers in our private chapel every morning at nine o'clock. The family sat on one side of the aisle and the staff on the other. This practice continued until the Second World War but was not reinstated after peace was declared. The Campbells had three children, two daughters and a son, who were friends of ours. It is a sad story for their parents, as they all three married, all three divorced and all were childless, and all eventually died of drink.

It is splendid that there is relatively little snobbery amongst the young. Occasionally, you still find a few snobs amongst the 'country' families, but otherwise to marry a black man, say, is considered perfectly all right. It is wonderful how the parents seem to have adapted themselves to this complete volte-face in society of today. Of course it is still fun to be asked to ducal residences, not so much because of the dukes as

A family group at Wilton House. The author's grandmother, the Dowager Countess of Pembroke, is seated in the centre; his sister, the Dowager Viscountess Hambleden, is seated left, with her second son Michael on her knee; on the right is Mary, Countess of Pembroke, with her baby daughter Diana; Henry, Viscount Hambleden, stands at the back of the group

because they have such beautiful houses filled with such glorious pictures and furniture. The opening to the public of these places has brought the different classes much nearer to each other than one would have thought possible fifty years ago. The National Trust has done a great job in preserving such architectural gems by taking them over from the families who have lived in them for centuries but can no longer afford to keep them up. These families endow them and so are allowed to live in some part of the house *ad infinitum.*

I have many great-nieces and -nephews and I am happy to say that not one of them is remotely snobbish. Their boy-friends or girl-friends come from every class in the British Isles. As long as they are intelligent, interesting or amusing, the parents will accept and welcome them into the family home. Inevitably there will always be a class system, but every year it is watered down and I hope one day will be of no importance and resentment will disappear.

Don't be a name-dropper – it is so tiresome and fools no one. For example. I have heard people say: 'As my great friend "Somerset" said to me', and so forth. No one ever called Somerset Maugham anything but 'Willie'. Equally, no one ever called Sacheverell Sitwell anything but 'Sashy'. It's not worth the risk of making a fool of yourself by trying to impress people. Certain Christian names are spelt differently from the way they are pronounced, which is another trap to be avoided. Loelia, for example, is pronounced Lelia.

Social climbing is an understandable fault – many people want to know the 'famous' who are always appearing in the glossy magazines – but in the end, where does it get you? If you don't belong to that set, you are never really part of it.

If you are a car snob and have bought the most

expensive and luxurious car on the market, don't put a bunch of flowers in an embossed silver cornucopia attached to the window separating you from the driver, for it is a sure sign of the *nouveaux riches*. An example was the ostentatious Lady Docker, whose Daimler had gold embellishments, and I expect her cornucopia was gold as well!

Don't grow up thinking that having good manners is unimportant. Exactly the opposite is the case. People will say 'What good manners he or she has got, isn't it refreshing', if one always gets up when an older person, man or woman, enters a room. We were very strictly brought up by my mother and I am eternally grateful to her. Even to this day, my sister aged eighty-seven will rise to her feet and not sit down until the visitor has done so. I am the same; sometimes, at eighty-three, I wish I didn't have to rise from a low chair to greet someone, but it is so ingrained in me that I suppose I do it automatically.

Some people have a habit, a bad habit, of moving one's furniture which one has carefully placed in positions where people can talk easily to each other. Another infuriating trick is throwing cushions on the floor! No one is allowed to come into my dining-room with a cigarette in his mouth. After the main course my guests can smoke if they like, but I would rather they waited until after the pudding. Another form of bad manners is being condescending and patronizing. It makes my blood boil when I hear someone being patronized who hasn't got the nerve to answer back. I suspect, though the person in question wouldn't admit it, that it comes from an inferiority complex which he is trying to cover up by being 'Mr Know-all'.

If you are a man, you should never go out of a room ahead of a woman. Always step aside and let her pass first, unless you are the host and have to lead the way.

Going to the drinks' tray and helping yourself to a whisky or whatever without asking the host is thoroughly bad manners. Again, helping yourself to wine at lunch or dinner without being invited by the host is 'not done'. Wait to be asked to help yourself and the other guests if there is no waiter to serve it. When you read this, you will probably say: 'Silly old buffer, what the hell does he think he's talking about?' But do think just the same, for it is so agreeable to be with good-mannered people.

Two examples of really good manners were, firstly, the late Duke of Kent who was giving a dinner party in his Belgrave Square house for a couple called the Lawson Johnsons. She was American and known as 'Little Betty'. She referred to the Prince of Wales and the Duke of Kent as 'my boys'. Mr Lawson Johnson was English and very impressed by his wife's grand friends. Whenever the Duke opened his mouth, whether what he said was funny or not, Mr Lawson Johnson would throw back his head and roar with laughter. The dining-room chairs were exquisite Chippendale. We went into dinner and Mr Lawson Johnson was placed next to the Duchess, with his back to the fireplace. At a certain moment there was a loud crack, drowning his laughter; the carved back of his chair shot into the fire and was totally destroyed. A terrible silence followed, and then the Duke in his charming manner said: 'It's quite all right. It's lucky it was the one chair that was not original. There were only eleven when I bought the set and this one was the copy I had made to complete the twelve.'

Freda Dudley Ward, afterwards Marquise de Casa Maury, was an exquisite, intelligent woman. She looked very fragile, with beautiful tiny bones. She was staying for a weekend with me at my house in the Park at Wilton and Reine Pitman, the niece of John Singer Sargent, the painter, brought over a famous Italian sculptress for drinks. The sculptress was a very masculine type of lady and took a great shine to Freda. On leaving, she took Freda's hand and gave it a great squeeze. Freda smiled and said how fascinating it was to meet such a wonderful sculptress. The woman left, after which Freda, rather pale, said: 'Darling, could you ring the local doctor. That Italian lady has broken my little finger.'

Be polite and considerate to whoever works for you at your home or serves you in shops or waits on you in restaurants; in fact, anyone who serves you, no matter in what capacity. The word servant has become almost a dirty word. This is a pity because to serve, literally speaking, means to help. This reminds me of Lady Cunard, Emerald to her friends, who had a lady's maid called Hudson. Hudson had been with her for a great many years and always addressed her as 'Milady'; they were friends as well as mistress and employee. During the last war, Emerald, American by birth but British by marriage, went to New York and stayed at the Ritz Hotel. One morning Hudson brought in her breakfast and said: 'It's a lovely day, Lady Cunard.' Emerald was surprised to be addressed in this manner and asked why. Hudson replied: 'Servants don't exist in this country unless they are black.' 'Nonsense,' said Emerald. 'That little maid who is white and does your room in this hotel is your servant. You are my servant. I am the servant of the King and he is the servant of God. So just get on with your work.'

Hudson remained with Emerald until she died many years later.

I am lucky with the Moroccans who serve me – they are part of the family. My cook and his wife have been with me for over thirty years – my butler/driver and gardener, fourteen and twelve respectively. There is no servility between us and because of our relationship the house has a truly happy atmosphere. In life you get what you give. Some people are unable to keep staff for more than a month or two. This is because they are inconsiderate and don't treat their employees as human beings.

The butler at Wilton, 'Mr Smith' to us children, was a splendid character. Every morning he would go to my mother's sitting-room for orders. It was amusing to hear them talking together. Perhaps one day at the end of a discussion, Smith, who had made some mistake, would say: 'I stand corrected, Milady.' Another day, if my mother was proved wrong, she would say: 'I stand corrected, Smith.' To sum it all up, they had a perfect relationship and deep respect for each other. Rudeness to servants, who can't answer back, is unforgivable; but in the end those who commit it, suffer for it.

If you feel like taking revenge on someone who has said unpleasant things about you or done unpleasant things to hurt you, don't, for it usually backfires. It is wiser to ignore it or laugh it off. Make them look silly if you can but don't be vindictive, for it makes you as bad as them.

My form of revenge was rather strange. It happened that someone I loved very much left me for someone else, as a consequence of which I was unhappy for several years. One day, to my astonishment, I discovered a small red leather box hidden behind a chest of drawers. I opened it and found literally dozens of love letters, all addressed to my former friend. I read them all. I then replaced them in the box and walked out on

The author as a young man, in his garden

to the roof terrace of my house. I took out my cigarette-lighter and burned the lot, a sort of funeral pyre. I waited until the last ash was blown away by the east wind. It was like being exorcized and completely cured my unhappiness and the hatred I had felt for so long. Would you call that revenge? I wonder, but at any rate it hurt no one, although the two people who were the source of my unhappiness did separate soon after.

To return to Lady Cunard, one evening a group of us were sitting on the piazza in Venice, including her and Sir Thomas Beecham. Sir Thomas was holding forth on the amount of mangy cats to be found in the streets of that city. He said that they should all be exterminated. Suddenly he was interrupted by a young American, whom no one knew, who had joined our table. He, in a falsetto voice, said: 'Do you mean, Sir Thomas, that if you saw a little titty bitty, little kitty drowning in the Grand Canal you wouldn't jump in and save it?' Sir Thomas, scarlet in the face, said: 'Young man, if I saw a titty bitty little kitty. . . . He got no further as Emerald, putting up her lorgnette, said: 'Oh my dear, who asked this young man on to the piazza?'

# 2

'What a pleasure it is to be with someone who looks on the bright side of things, especially when something goes wrong. Cheer up a person if you can by turning the misadventure into a funny incident, such as missing your connection during an air flight, or your car breaking down on a lonely road. I think I am rather good at that, or so Richard Tinewell of Sotheby's tells me. Three years ago he and I and Celia Stuart, a great friend (alas, she died recently), were stuck in the airport at Dakar in Senegal for seven hours. The people there were odious, and the bank slammed its shutters down in our faces although it wasn't closing-time for another five minutes. We had no money except a few pounds. We asked what should we do with our luggage – a shrug of the shoulders and the porter walked away. Eventually we found a place to leave our bags, which cost us our last pennies. Every time we inquired when our plane would arrive to take us to Freetown in Sierra Leone, the reply was: 'No idea. Perhaps this evening, perhaps tomorrow.'

I decided to turn the whole thing into a huge joke, trying to be funny and amuse the other two, and in the end we were all laughing, if somewhat hysterically. At last the plane, Air Africa, tied together with string, arrived. We had had nothing to eat or drink, but we made it. On arrival, chaos. We were surrounded by bunches of little black men pushing and shoving to get our custom and expecting a tip. Luckily the hotel had sent someone to meet us, so he paid out what was necessary, for which in due course we reimbursed him. At last, after about an hour, we climbed into a rickety helicopter and were deposited at our hotel. I love that hotel, but it is not super-luxurious. The lights go out at ten, as they are not on the mains and use a generator of their own. At least we got something to eat, but I could see by their faces that my poor friends were far from pleased. I prayed God that the next morning, when they saw the beach that I loved, the warm, gentle sea, the sweetness of the natives, the delicious exotic fruit, the palm trees, the fishermen, the women with baskets on their heads carrying pawpaw, pineapples, mangoes and so forth, they would love it. They did. They really loved it and we spent a blissful two weeks there. The return trip, again via Dakar, was planned so that we could stay with Mark Gilbey on the island of Goré. The same little plane flew us there and out of kindness, because of course we were hours late, didn't bother to land at the usual stops in Guinea and Gambia, because, as the pilot said: 'It's not worth it. There are so few people, they can wait there until we return tomorrow.' On arrival at Dakar, owing to the inefficiency of the Customs and police, we missed the last boat to Goré and had to spend the night at the hotel, kindly paid for by Mark.

To be an optimist is a real gift. Luckily for me, I was born one. I am always sure that everything will turn out all right although, heavens knows, half the time it doesn't. I am still as optimistic as ever about the future. I can't imagine going through life being pessimistic, with nothing to look forward to, always expecting the worst. For me, it would make life not worth living. There is no cure for it, as it is part of your make-up. I suppose, if you are a pessimist and you have known nothing else, it doesn't worry you as much as it would me.

Being a 'lion-hunter', meaning getting all the most important people to your house, makes you, oddly enough, into a figure of fun. Lady Colefax was the perfect example of such a person – not so much for the society folk she gathered round her as for the writers, artists and such like, though royalty was the exception. Once at Sunday luncheon, Lord Berners thought he would play a joke on poor Sybil. He rang up and said that the P of W (Prince of Wales) was coming that Sunday and would she like to come? 'Oh, my dear, I am supposed to go somewhere else but I'll put it off.' We were all assembled in the drawing-room having a drink when Gerald announced that luncheon was ready. Sybil said: 'Oh, but where is the P of W?' 'Over there,' said Gerald, pointing to the Provost of Worcester. Apart from her little weakness, Lady Colefax, who started the decorating business Colefax & Fowler, was a nice woman and, when you were alone with her, she was charming company. She was the niece of Miss Jekyll, the famous gardener, She once told me how as a little girl Miss Jekyll had said to her that, perhaps when she grew up and married, she would have a garden. Remember one thing: 'Take care of your nose in a garden and your eyes will take care of themselves.' She lived to a great age, by which time she was bent double with arthritis. One day Osbert Sitwell, who disliked her and would never accept her invitations, said that he was walking down Lord North Street one morning and thought he saw some children bowling a hoop along the pavement. He looked again and found it was Lady Colefax. Another time someone said to him, 'Good morning, Osbert, how are you today?' 'Terrible,' he said. 'I saw Lady Colefax through glass.'

If you grow up to be greedy, you'll have a hard time to check the urge. If the sight of a cake or an ice-cream makes your mouth water, even though you have just had an enormous lunch or dinner, it means that your eyes are bigger than your stomach. This organ can't take gluttony, your digestion will be upset and you will grow fatter and fatter. The first rule is to will yourself not to nibble between meals. If you have any will-power, this should not be too difficult. The second rule is always to refuse a second helping. Ask your real friends to say: 'Now then, Jemima, remember what Great-Uncle David said.' Other friends, half in fun, say: 'Oh go on, have some more, you're not really all that fat.' Another thing: try to eat slowly. Don't gulp everything down without masticating. Look at yourself in the mirror as often as you can, preferably a long mirror and, little by little, with any luck, you will be appalled by what you see. That is the moment to make a stupendous effort and go on a diet. If you are strong-minded enough and have enough vanity to want to attract young men, this should do the trick. The alternative is to find a man who likes fat girls. There are quite a lot of these fellows around, in which case you can marry one and happily get larger and larger. Such a man will say: 'How marvellous. All this is mine.'

Being a drunk is a much worse fault. You lose what looks you've got, become puffy round the eyes, develop a double chin, become slovenly and untidy and, worst of all, your hair becomes greasy and your make-up smudged. In fact, you come to look a real mess. Try Alcoholics Anonymous, or marry a man who has the same trouble as you: he won't ever worry what a mess you look.

Lady Aberconway, Christabel to her friends, though

Cecil Barr with her fiancé, Morocco, 1937

not an alcoholic, decidedly drank too much. She was very gentle and carried it off fairly well. A good example is the following. I was training to be a wireless operator at the beginning of the last war at a college in Llandudno. Christabel's house, called Bodnant (Lord Aberconway had made a wonderful garden which was visited by thousands of people every year), was quite close. Their son John McLaren married my first cousin Lady Rose Paget, and one day when I was lunching with them Christabel said: 'Rose darling, will you fetch me my glass of orange juice on the table over there.' There were several glasses of the same liquid and Rose picked up the nearest one and took a great gulp. 'Good God, what's this? It tastes awful.' Christable in her precise, elegant voice said: 'Rose, that glass has whisky mixed with the orange juice. Whisky is medicinal and your mother-in-law has been ordered whisky by her doctor, so kindly fill it with the same amount of whisky you have just swallowed. Never, never touch my glass again. You know perfectly well it is a different shape to the others.' Alas, she steadily got worse and in the end was asked to very few houses, as she was always falling about.

Men seem to get away with being drunk from time to time, but in a woman it is extremely unattractive.

Another woman, my aunt Lady Victor Paget, became a drunk in later life. Frequently she had to be carried home paralytic at the end of an evening. I used to stay with her in her London house, and having seen Aunt Bridget coming home plastered night after night, I was amazed that she never had a hangover. She would wake me early in the morning and I would go down to the dining-room and find her devouring fish cakes and bacon – and bright as a button. How lucky she was! She was the one I mentioned in *Engaging*

*Eccentrics* who had her face lifted so often that the last time she went to 'my little woman round the corner', as she called her, she was told: 'I'm sorry, Lady Victor, but there's nothing left to lift.'

During the last war I inherited Boyton Manor, after the death of my cousin Sidney Herbert. The local clergyman was a drunkard and the parishioners longed to get rid of him. The only possible way would be if he were to be caught drunk in the pulpit. But he was far too cunning to fall into that trap. As he got older I suppose he had less will-power and I received this message from our representative when I was in Australia, where my ship was in dock: 'Glad to inform you the Revd so-and-so dismissed. Last Sunday he got up in the pulpit and shouted: "On your knees you bitches and buggers."'

I am lucky that I have never had the least inclination to drink to excess. I know exactly when to stop. It's just 'the one over the odds' that does it, after which you have no idea how many you have had and become incredibly boring. You keep repeating yourself all the time, either getting aggressive or tearful, but worst of all is to become maudlin and amorous. The next day you feel ghastly and remember nothing about the night before. Is it really worth it?

When I was young, drugs rarely existed except amongst a small set in London – Brenda Dean Paul, Kit Preston, Tomy Sardiellas, names of the past, were the most famous. Occasionally for a thrill people used to sniff cocaine, but they seldom became addicted. Tallulah Bankhead, far from being addicted, used to say: 'Darling, would you like to try some "uppies", as she called them. 'It's not habit-forming, you know.' And with her it certainly wasn't. She really did it to keep up her reputation of being wicked.

It is unfair that Morocco has the reputation of being a country where drugs flourish. I know a great many people of every nationality and in every walk of life, and unless I am being remarkably naïve, to my knowledge none of them takes drugs. The local people grow marijuana purely for 'export'. The business thrives because so many tourists – English, American, Swedish and German – come to Morocco to buy it cheap and attempt to smuggle it out of the country to sell in Europe at a vast profit. The gaols here are full of such people, and unless their families bail them out they remain incarcerated for many years. I have no sympathy for them, because they seldom purchase drugs for purely personal use. In fact they are simply pushers. None the less, the drug situation is infinitely worse in Europe and the United States than it is in Morocco.

When you are eighteen and lack confidence, it is probably the fault of your parents, who have not bothered with you during your adolescent years, leaving you to fend for yourself and struggle alone into womanhood. Perhaps you spent those formative years with people inferior to you mentally – in fact, anyone who will listen to your troubles and say: 'There, there, you will grow out of it when you are older.' Then from one day to the next your parents begin to notice you and start thinking of what they are going to do with you. Obviously the first thought is to marry you off, but it's all very well their expecting this to be easy. No doubt they don't realize that, unwittingly, they have given you an inferiority complex, as you have never met the sort of young man from their background whom, they hope, you will attract – and vice versa. You have no conversation and feel completely at sea arriving at certain parties or a dance. You watch other girls laughing away completely sure of themselves while you tremble with embarrassment and become a kind of 'deaf mute'. Eventually you give up and make friends elsewhere and probably marry or live with a young man who is undesirable in the eyes of your parents. If this happens and you are happy, forget the past and make a new life with a totally different set of friends from what your parents expected of you. If your parents don't approve, it is just too bad, but you must say to yourself: 'To hell with them, I'm happy, I've gained self-confidence and I'm looking forward to my life ahead.' I know several young women like this, but being very fond of the parents I shall keep their names a secret!

If you grow up and want to be an actor but can't act, you must satisfy this passion by being permanently on-stage in everyday life. People might say 'She is such a poseur', little knowing that you can't live without acting. It is cruel to be born with a trait that causes you to be considered 'affected'. In my own case I managed to come to terms with it by acting, not very well, in two films directed by Elinor Glyn. I realized at once that I wasn't good enough to carry on, so contented myself by playing as many parts as I possibly could in amateur theatricals. This satisfied my passion for the stage. I usually played the Dame or one of the Ugly Sisters in pantomimes. I also acted and sometimes directed sketches in revues, presented in Tangier in aid of local charities.

When you get older you will find that people are fascinated by the past. They will listen avidly to your anecdotes and accounts of amusing situations in which you have found yourself through the years. This is gratifying and in some ways, in my case, compensates for my never having been a success in the theatre. In fact it is a form of being on-stage. One of the pitfalls of getting old is repeating yourself. You must make sure, when you begin a story, that you have not told your particular audience the same one before. You can pretty well tell when you start by the look on their faces and quickly change the subject if necessary. I am lucky that at eighty-three I have not lost my marbles and my memory is, thank God, as clear as it ever was.

Unfortunately, I have lost the sight of one eye by contracting glaucoma. The good one is still fairly sound, but I have to put endless drops in morning and night and swallow pills, which make one go to the loo much too often. I can read and drive my car in the daytime but must be careful going down steps, as they seem to disappear and all too easily I can fall headlong on the floor or down garden paths. The worst are badly lit staircases in apartment houses and also dim lights in drawing-rooms and dining-rooms. Nothing can be done; you just have to live with it. It does make one less inclined to go out to large dinner parties in houses or flats that one doesn't know well. My advice is if you feel there is something not quite right about your eyes and changing spectacles doesn't help, go at once to the oculist and he will stop it getting worse. Regrettably, I didn't catch it in time, thinking: Oh, it's probably my liver. Incidentally, the disease is con-genital and so far no cure has been found for it. I am sure there will be one day, but that will come a little late for me.

The other day I was lunching with the painter Claudio Bravo. Marguerite McBey, also a painter, was there. She has lost her sense of balance, and as we were leaving we said simultaneously: 'Look at us, two old crocks – you can't walk and I can't see. We are a pretty pair, aren't we?'

*41*

(*L to r*) The author, Poppet John, Lady Diana Cooper,
*c.* 1936

My Aunt 'Frid', my mother's elder sister, was a very beautiful woman. She was shy and retiring and had the face of an angel. A marriage was arranged for her at an early age by my grandmother. The bridegroom was Lord Ingestre, the future Earl of Shrewsbury, the premier earl of England. This was because my mother had already married well and my grandmother was furious that 'Frid' had not been snapped up first. She adored this daughter and didn't care so much for my mother. Poor Aunt Frid wasn't the least in love with 'Uncle', as we called him, but dutifully gave him three daughters and a son. He was killed early in the 1914–18 war. Later she married an American diplomat, Richard Panoyer, whom she adored. They had one son, 'Kim', who has spent much of his life in Kenya arranging safaris for visiting American and English tourists.

Aunt Frid was a 'Mrs Malaprop'. She always got her phrases wrong. For instance, one day we went into the optician's shop in Salisbury, which was run by a respectable old man called Mr Hamblin. Aunt Frid went up to the counter and said: 'Good morning, Mr Hamblin. I would like a pair of bisexual glasses, if you please.' Horror on the face of the old man. I quickly chipped in: 'Bifocal, Mr Hamblin. Bifocal, please.' Another time Kim had hiccups and Aunt Frid was heard to say: "Drink your breath and hold your water.' She arrived for a weekend at Wilton and walked into the library with a bandage on her nose. My mother said: 'Darling, what's happened to your nose?' 'Oh, I had it castrated,' replied Frid, meaning of course cauterized. I had been working in the United States for a few years and one evening, after my return, she was staying at Wilton and whispered to me, just before we were all going to bed: 'Come to my room, darling, I want to ask you something.' I dutifully went and said: 'What do you want to ask me, darling?' She replied: 'Is it true that niggers can kick them aside like a train?' Such a wonderfully Edwardian turn of phrase – I mean the train! All these remarks were made doubly funny coming from her seraphic face.

# 3

If you grow up to be a horsy girl, try not to fall in love with a bookworm or someone who likes town life and can bear the country only for weekends. Don't think you can change that person's habits; it's much better to break it off as quickly as possible. I know of a case, admittedly the other way round, when a great neighbour of mine loved a horsy girl and even took up riding to please her, though he didn't much like it. She eventually broke up their relationship and I said to him: 'You are well out of it, if she would rather live with a horse than with you.'

Don't wait too long before you marry. So often these days, young couples live together and think: Oh well, we will get married later. But time passes and suddenly they find they don't love each other any more. They separate, as there are no children to keep them together. By that time they are probably around thirty and it's not that easy to find a husband, so they go from one lover to another until it's too late. That's how to end up a childless woman alone or a woman alone with a fatherless child.

It is easy to say that marriage should be based on compatibility rather than sex. But most people fall in love for the latter and, when the sexual attraction fades, realize that they have absolutely nothing in common, so naturally they drift apart. They do not necessarily divorce but lead their own separate lives and stick together for the sake of the children.

In the old days most marriages were 'arranged', and

perhaps it wasn't such a bad idea. Divorce was unheard of and after so many years the husband had a mistress and the wife a lover. The 'home life' went on just the same: the children had no idea of these goings-on and grew up in blissful ignorance. Needless to say, there were quite a few illegitimate offspring.

If you grow up to be soft-hearted, remember that some people will take advantage of your gentle nature, so choose your friends carefully. I am thinking of years gone by, when English aristocrats had become, for one reason or another, impoverished. These 'gentlemen' sailed away to America to find a rich bride whose parents were probably delighted that their daughter should become a duchess, a marchioness, a countess or even a viscountess. These poor girls were forced into loveless marriage. In particular, Consuelo Vanderbilt, the sweetest of women who had the hell of a life with the Duke of Marlborough. Although she dutifully bore him two sons, she eventually could bear it no longer and, because of her vast fortune, managed to have the marriage anulled. She then married Jacques Balsain, a French Catholic, and lived happily with him for many years in a lovely house in the South of France.

Today, a girl doesn't marry someone just because she is told to do so by her parents. But still, look out, especially if you are rich, because there are always fortune-hunters around. Poor Barbara Hutton was a perfect example of this. She once said to me: 'Darling, I was pretty, wasn't I? Yet no one married me for love. I can never think why.' I said: 'Because no decent man would propose to you, as the world would say: "He is only after your money."' Sad but true. I have known many heiresses and it is always the same story. Divorce after divorce, as they seek the happiness they seldom if ever find.

Alice Astor was another great heiress. Her mother Mrs John Jacob Astor, married secondly Lord Ribblesdale, himself a widower. So Alice was brought up in England. She had first married Prince Serge Obolensky, by whom she had a son and a daughter. She then married Raimund von Hofmannsthal, grandson of the great Hofmannsthal, and had two daughters. Thirdly she married an Englishman, David Pleydell-Bouverie, but had no children by him, and lastly Philip Harding, by whom she had one daughter. All four marriages ended in tears. She died in New York still a fairly young woman. I loved her and miss her to this day.

If you find out that your husband is bisexual, in some ways it can be a relief. The reason that a friend of mine gave was that when the physical side of their marriage was over she was worried that some other woman would take him away, whereas if it is another man it will certainly not break up the marriage. In fact such a situation can make a married couple feel more secure.

Another friend of mine discovered affectionate letters to her husband written on BEA notepaper. She feared they were from an air hostess. When she broached the subject, he replied: 'Oh, they are from a pilot.' She told me she breathed a sigh of relief!

If you marry and discover that you are unable to have children, obviously you will be very unhappy for a time. You have been to all the doctors for medical advice and so has your husband, with no result. You then discuss the situation together and decide to adopt a child. I have known several similar cases. Some have turned out successful, some have not, but it is certainly worthwhile to take the risk. The most difficult moment comes when you feel you must tell the child that he or

A party group, *c.* 1935. (*L to r*) The author, his brother
Sidney (Lord Herbert), Cecil Beaton, Lady Caroline Paget,
Chips Channon, Bebé Berard

she is adopted. Some children take it quite calmly; others mind dreadfully. But it's better to be told by your so-called father or mother than by anyone else later in life. Naturally, if you are grown up, you become curious as to who your real parents were and it probably becomes an obsession and worries you for the rest of your life.

It is quite understandable how many marriages are successful when two people are mentally attuned. My advice to the young is not to stick to your generation only. Make friends with people older and younger than yourself. The older generation can teach you a great deal of wisdom, and the younger generation will listen to what you have to tell them. And of course by making friends with people of different ages, you need never be lonely. Naturally, your contemporary friends are irreplaceable and most of them have probably already died, but with luck your younger ones will see you through.

I was exceptionally lucky in this way. I would listen entranced to conversation between intellectuals such as Lady Ottoline Morrell, Osbert Sitwell, Lord David Cecil and many others. This was made possible by the existence of Miss Edith Olivier, an aunt of Laurence Olivier. She was a well-known authoress and lived in the Daye House in the Park at Wilton, given to her for life by my father. Every kind of painter, sculptor, writer and poet would motor down at weekends to spend happy hours in her company. She always welcomed me and I would sit, silent as a mouse, entranced by the brilliant conversation going on around me. I benefited a great deal from the kindness of Edith, who gave me a sort of education I should never have had otherwise.

As I became older, I made a point of making new

friends younger than myself and now I am surrounded by friends of all ages. Practically none of my contemporaries is still alive, but I am never lonely. It is no fun being old, but at least the young help one to keep on the ball mentally.

Don't expect too much of your children and grandchildren, and above all don't pretend that they are all perfect, that all your geese are swans. Grandmothers are apt to do this, and spoil them outrageously, much to the annoyance of the parents who are trying hard to discipline them. Of course grandchildren take advantage of this, knowing full well that the parents will shrug their shoulders and give up when Granny is around!

If you never get married but have ambition and a certain ability, become a career girl. Otherwise I don't know what to suggest, except perhaps, if you like animals, start a kennel where people leave their pets while holidaying abroad. Open a small antique shop in a country town, preferably on the tourist route or start a tea-shop in some seaside resort. If your father dies first, don't be dominated by a selfish mother, who will ruin your life by complaining that you have no time for her and don't love her any more, or some such rubbish. I have known several girls who have suffered in this way and, after their mothers have died, have been left pretty well on their own because they have lost their friends through their mothers' refusal to invite them to the house or, when they did come, by spending the entire time nagging.


What if you grow up to be ostentatious and are a show-off, what do you do? Obviously you don't realize you are either of those things. Someone who is fond of you should point them out to you, but who would like to take on this unpleasant task? You certainly would not listen to your parents – in fact it is entirely up to you. If you are observant, you will see a look of boredom and a lifting of the eyebrows on the faces of those around you, should you for instance contradict them flat and then continue to expound on the subject, listening to no one who may try to interrupt you. The worst is knowing the 'dates' of every king, every battle and the rest. Jane Bowles once silenced someone who was going on and on. He turned to Janie and said: 'Aren't I right?' She replied: 'I am sure you are, but for me there is nothing deader than history!' Of course she was far too clever and erudite to mean it literally; but it certainly silenced the offender. So do remember that no one likes being given a lecture by another. If you go voluntarily to a meeting where a professional lecturer is talking about some subject in which you are interested, that is a different matter.

I have reached the time of life when I honestly don't care any more what people say or think about me. I used to mind very much, but growing a thick skin is about the only compensation of old age. This does not come from conceit but, with so little time left, what is the point of minding? Perhaps also human beings have a certain respect for old people. It suddenly makes them think: Oh dear, perhaps I shall be like that one day. I do hope people will be nice and kind to me.

Diana Cooper was bedridden for the last year or so of her long life – she died some five years ago at ninety-three – but she was loved by so many people younger than herself that she was never alone. Lying in bed, still beautiful with her little chihuahua called Doggie on the pillow beside her, she would reminisce for a short while and then fall asleep. The last time I saw her, she said: 'The thing I mind most is that I don't recognize the names of anyone in power today. I am completely out of touch with the world, so I am bored, bored, bored. . . .' It was pathetic, but for someone who had been in the public eye for nearly a century, it was a perfectly natural reaction. It is hard to believe that she would be ninety-eight if she was still alive and that I shall be eighty-four on my next birthday. It makes me feel, in a silly way, that I am catching up with her. I had always thought of myself as so much younger!

There are people who are boring and there are people who are bores – two different things. By boring people I mean those who are dull and have little to say. Whereas bores have too much to say and bang on like a woodpecker until you are at the end of your tether. You find yourself being rude to them, not out of unkindness but from sheer exhaustion. They tell long-winded stories, one after the other, prefacing each with the remark 'Stop me if I've told you this before', and then go on without a pause for you to say 'Yes.' This fault stems from a total lack of sensitivity – hence the expression 'He's the club bore.' He will sit at his club waiting for some newcomer to buttonhole, who will probably fall asleep after about an hour, unable to make a get-away without being plain rude. Often these unfortunate people are retired Anglo-Indian colonels and the like who live on a pension, are lonely and probably widowers, so they can exist only on stories of their Empire-building past. Another form of bore is the one who tells endless dirty stories after dinner over the port. Thank God these breeds are dying out!

Some women don't seem to mind if you don't listen to their stories, as long as you say now and then: 'Oh really', 'No, fancy that!', 'How fascinating'. You can simply switch off and think of other things, while they go happily prattling on.

Lady Halick, a sister of the late Duchess of Devonshire, was slightly deaf. She invented a wonderful way of coping with bores. If she saw one approaching, she would switch off her machine, point to her ears, smile sweetly and move away.

If you are deaf or blind you certainly realize it. What is lucky for bores is that they have no idea they are bores!

When you say someone is lacking in charm, what do you really mean? How can one describe charm? It certainly has nothing to do with beauty. Some ugly people have so much charm that you entirely forget their looks. It must be a thing of the spirit, something inside you that shines a sort of beam of good nature, interest and welcome. People are apt to say 'I fell completely under her or his charm', which really means that they can't quite understand why. Lucky are those born with such a gift, as I think it the most enviable thing in the world to possess. I shall not mention names here because people who are ugly would mind very much, as I don't believe anyone sees themselves as they appear to others. Naturally, if you have a squint or a harelip you are conscious of it, but modern surgery is so wonderful that almost any deformity can be remedied, even to remodelling a face badly disfigured in some accident or other. Of all the progress that has been made in this century I consider that medical work is far and away the most miraculous and important development. When you consider the longevity of life for the average person today, compared with the old days, when to reach the age of seventy was a record and at sixty you were considered very old indeed and well on the way out.

On the terrace at Wilton House. The author with (*from right to left*) the Countess of Pembroke, his great-nephew William and his great-niece Jemima

# 4

When I was a little boy, as with most privileged children of my generation, I hardly knew my parents. They were figureheads, to be respected and feared. We – my brothers, sister and I – probably saw them twice a day. We were sent into our mother's bedroom after breakfast to say 'good-morning' and again brought down to the drawing-room after tea to say 'good-night'. The rest of the day was spent in the nursery or the schoolroom; not until we reached the age of about twelve did we eat in the dining-room – and then at a separate table. We hardly opened our mouths except to gobble up the food and waited patiently for my mother to tell us when we could leave the room. Today at Wilton we all eat together, irrespective of ages; in fact, the other day we were about eighteen people, ranging from me in my eighties to my great-niece Jemima, aged two and a half.

I don't think we suffered from being separated from the grown-ups. We took it for granted, but it did mean that we hardly got to know our parents at all until we were adolescents. My elder brother Sidney and my younger brother Anthony disliked my mother, while my sister and I on the other hand were devoted to her. No one could say that she was actually a bad mother, since we wanted for nothing. We had our ponies, our dogs and our bicycles, and were sent to the seaside every summer to a rented house. We were also sent abroad to learn languages and all the rest of the things that children of the well-off did in those days. To sum it up, I suppose my mother was not a maternal woman in the recognized sense of the word.

All this has changed because nursery governesses and French governesses no longer exist, and nannies barely do, and so the parents have to look after their children themselves, whether they like it or not.

I remember once there was a dance going on in the servants' hall. We children decided to join the party, so, when we were supposed to be in bed, we crept down the nursery tower stairs and joined the fun. We were caught. Our punishment was to be sent early to bed the following evening, and without supper. My father, the kindest of men, slunk upstairs with a plate of food for us. He was caught in the act by my mother and severely reprimanded! Owing to his gentle and somewhat retiring character, my mother had to take up the reins and run Wilton and the estate herself. My Uncle Charlie, her brother, the Marquess of Anglesey, told me that, as a girl, she was a regular tomboy, full of fun and laughter. She realized that she had to change because my father had no wish to run anything – he just liked fishing, shooting and making bonfires. So my poor mother became 'the boss'. She was on all local committees, was Mayor of Wilton three times, worked on the county council, ran the Salisbury Infirmary – in fact, to all intents and purposes, she became the Earl of Pembroke. She once said to me: 'Darling, isn't it unfair that I should have worked so hard all my life and am now respected and perhaps admired, while Daddy, who has done nothing, is absolutely adored by everyone?'

I am surprised that the children of famous people appear to mind so little about the biographies of their parents. The lives of Lord and Lady Mountbatten is a good example of this, revealing sides of their characters which were unknown during their lifetimes except by a very small circle. It seems that to denigrate people in any possible way is the current fashion; knocking heroes off their pedestals is apparently great fun. I suspect that, in their hearts, the children do mind but feel that if they made a fuss it would become a public scandal, so it is best to leave it alone.

Another example of this kind of thing was a long article in an American magazine about Lady Kenmare. It was thoroughly unpleasant and uncalled for. I was very fond of her and am sorry that I even talked to the man who wrote it. She has two children living, a son and a daughter both happily married, and I am sure they mind very much, as Enid, whatever her faults, was a good and devoted mother.

How to get over an infirmity: If, in later years, you are disfigured by some accident, it is bad enough for an ordinary person. If you are an actor, it should be a real disaster – but not so for Esmé Percy, a well-known and much-loved character actor who had an eye bitten out by his beloved spaniel. Instead of going under, he decided to make a joke of it. So he had several eyes made of different colours. On-stage he naturally used the one matching his real eye, but off-stage he would amuse himself and others by suddenly removing the matching one and slipping in either a ruby red one, a sapphire blue or an emerald green one – and then flash it at you! The effect was startling, to say the least, but he was such a funny man that we would roar with laughter at this grotesque joke.

There are certain people who make mischief or hurt other people's feelings unintentionally. This comes from not thinking before you speak. An amusing Canadian, Peggy Hulbrecht, married to a Dutchman, was one of these. Friends would say Peggy is great fun, entertains well and is very generous, but look out, because she's an awful bitch. One day Dan, her husband, said to me: 'Do try and persuade Peggy to think before she speaks.' I tried and Peggy said: 'But how can I? I don't know what I'm going to say until I've said it!' In fact, her censor cells were obviously missing when she was born. To think of going through life with this handicap sounds awful to us, but I don't believe for one moment that Peggy had any idea that people thought of her as a bitch.

Nobody knows what they are really like, however introspective they may be. Sometimes you may recognize a fault in another person and realize you have that same fault yourself. This may help you to correct it. I wonder how helpful it is to go to a psychoanalyst? It seems to me to resemble a Roman Catholic going to confession; I suppose it clears your conscience for the time being but it doesn't have a lasting effect. Most human beings like talking about themselves and in the two cases I have just quoted they certainly did that. Am I being too cynical? I hope not. Personally I prefer to bear the burden of guilt myself and to try to correct it in my own way. This is sometimes successful and sometimes not, but at least you are not bothering other people. I've known friends who for years have gone to a psychoanalyst and have got steadily worse. Lord Sudeley was such a case and eventually went pretty well round the bend. Others have seen the light and escaped in time, perhaps because the person they love has become ill and for the first time they think about another human being instead of only themselves. I have no right to condemn psychiatry, as in some cases it has proved highly successful, especially if you are by nature lonely and lack the ability to make friends. The psychiatrist will listen while you pour out your soul and rid yourself of the misery that you have bottled up all your life. I have a nephew who did just that. He is now married, with a son, and is one of the sweetest, kindest and happiest of men.

Try not to judge other people. We can't all be alike, so why bother? They have their friends and you have yours. 'I don't think I dislike anyone,' I remember Diana Cooper saying, 'but I don't want to see them, because they give me no pleasure.' That seems to me the perfect way of going through life.

Don't be ashamed of telling white lies. Often they are used to avoid hurting someone's feelings. I frequently tell them for this reason. Rather than say no, I can't lunch or dine, because I don't want to, I invent some excuse such as I've got a bad tummy or I've got friends arriving and I don't know exactly what time they will get here. To tell lies for the sake of telling them is another matter and to be avoided if possible, such as making up stories glorifying yourself or pretending to know famous people when you have never met them. You are nearly always caught out and in consequence look a complete fool.

# Elsie de Wolfe

# 5

Have you ever seen a ghost? I have. We were staying with my Aunt Frid – our Mrs Malaprop – at St Donat's, a very ancient castle in South Wales. It was supposed to be haunted, but to us children it was just an exciting place with manholes, cellars and all the things that go with a medieval castle. One evening my brother Sidney, my younger brother Tony my cousin Ursula and I were going through the long gallery on our way to have tea in the Great Hall with the grown-ups, when we saw a lady playing the piano. 'Who is it?' I whispered to Ursula. 'No idea,' she replied. The lady beckoned to us to come over. She did not speak, but smiled sweetly and went on playing. We gradually backed away and ran downstairs and asked Aunt Frid who the silent lady was, dressed in a long grey dress, playing the piano. Aunt Frid said: 'Oh, that's a lady who lives in the village. She can't afford a piano, so I have told her to come and use ours when she likes.' We thought no more about it.

Years later, Aunt Frid said: 'Do you remember when you, Ursula, Sidney and Tony saw the lady playing the piano in the long gallery at St Donat's? Well, all three of you saw the famous St Donat's ghost who was hacked to death by her drunken husband.'

Have you ever been invited to a house where you have never been before and, on arrival, know every inch of it, even to the bedroom where you last slept? It has happened to me twice in my life and it is an uncanny feeling, not frightening. On the contrary, it gives you hope for a future life, as surely you must have visited these places in a former existence. It is particularly curious that it should have happened to me, as I am not in the least psychic. I think my Aunt Frid must have been, since, when she was pregnant and sitting on the wall surrounding a cemetery with her cousin Polly Cotton, a cold hand from a grave touched her. She fainted, became desperately ill and then had a miscarriage.

Do you, or do I, believe in fortune-tellers? It is always difficult to answer that question. Undoubtedly certain individuals have this talent, but there are so many charlatans around who make their living out of gullible men and women, it makes one fight shy of any of them. On the other hand, non-professional people, who don't even think of themselves as fortune-tellers, often predict events well into the future. I must mention at this point General André Beaufre, whose widow Genevieve now lives in Tangier. I had been listening and watching on television the dramatic events in the Soviet Union that occurred in August 1991. The following day I lunched with Madame Beaufre and said to her: 'Do you remember about fifteen years ago André saying to me, 'I shan't be alive in the mid-eighties but you will, and believe me, communism will start to fall apart then, and by the early nineties it will collapse completely.' She had forgotten that her husband had made that prophecy, but when I reminded her, she remembered the incident clearly. So you see, it's impossible to disbelieve that some people can see into the future without all the rigmarole of crystal balls, table-turning and the like, in darkened rooms smelling of sickly incense.

Lucky are the men and women in this life who have no feeling of guilt, however unkind or wicked they have been. What happens in the next life nobody knows, but I have noticed that when they are near to death they are frightened. I feel real compassion for people who suffer from a terminal illness, but most of them seem to be serene and look forward to the end. I feel it doesn't matter when you die but how you die. That is my philosophy, but perhaps it's a selfish one.

There are, as we know, people who have a death wish, though they may be perfectly strong and healthy. These suicides, I can't understand them, for surely there is always something to live for? Apparently the wish to take your own life is quite common, brought on by marital stress or loneliness. It is a strange mixture of courage and cowardice: courage to commit the act; cowardice in not facing the future. In recent years one of my dearest friends, Lady Nutting, took her life. She was born Anne Gunning, a top model of the sixties. She was one of the loveliest women I have ever known – not only lovely but gentle, kind and considerate. When she died, we were all horrified and her poor husband was *distrait*. Why she decided she had had enough of this world no one will ever know, for she was only sixty years old, still beautiful and perfectly healthy. She had wonderful obituaries and left many loyal and loving friends. Somehow her suicide was never taken up by the media, and how this came about also remains a secret.

When you are an eighteen-year-old girl, don't cover your face with make-up. There is nothing lovelier than a smooth, natural complexion; in fact, the 'bloom of youth'. Wear pale lipstick and perhaps, if you are inclined to have a shiny nose, a touch of powder; otherwise, wait till you reach the age of thirty or so before you really make up. After sixty use less lipstick, less rouge and less eye-shadow because the latter make your wrinkles look deeper, and lipstick settles into the lines of your lips. Over-painted women of a certain age look like harridans and years older than they actually are. It's the same with clothes. When you are young, dress young. When you are middle-aged, don't try and dress young, such as by wearing very short skirts because it happens to be the fashion. You will simply look ridiculous. Worst of all is old women wearing trousers.

The same applies to elderly men who appear in terrible T-shirts, with large stomachs and a lot of hair sprouting from their chests or from under their arms. They look positively revolting. In fact you should, as you get older, dress discreetly, so as not to advertise your poor, misshapen body.

I hope you love all animals. I do also, birds and even reptiles. To me, a house devoid of some living creature is somehow rather dead. Mind you, this passion can be carried too far; for instance, when you can't find a chair to sit down on because you must not disturb the dog or cat, is tiresome. Also animals at mealtimes, which beg or push their nose – if a dog – into your elbow just as you are raising a spoonful of soup to your mouth. Or a cat which scratches your leg under the table, to draw attention to itself, so that you will give it something from your plate. You must remember that a great many people don't like animals at all. Personally, I prefer big dogs to little ones. My favourite breed is a chow. Years ago, in London, anyone owning a chow would, at eleven o'clock, let it out of the front door and not worry about it coming home, because the owner knew where it was going and how long it would be away. Such dogs gathered near the Serpentine in Hyde Park and would sit around, obviously discussing important events amongst themselves. It was known as the 'Chows' Parliament' and people would go and watch, fascinated by the strange spectacle. In those days there was much less traffic and London was much smaller. No skyscrapers existed in the centre of the city and there were no multi-storey hotels. Park Lane, so luxurious, was lined with private houses. Today it couldn't possibly happen; all dogs are kept on leads when they go out with their owners. I have had dogs all my life, but have now given them up. I have resorted to cats, for the simple reason that they look after themselves. Dogs need exercise; going for walks is essential to their happiness. Cats are independent, but no less affectionate for that. Once when I was departing from Tangier for two or three weeks in England, I left my suitcase, already packed, open in my bedroom. When I came out of the bathroom I found my white cat Snowflake in the suitcase, determined to travel with me!

When you are old, don't overdo it. You must realize that your constitution can't take the same amount of strain as it did before, so don't force it. Try and take a siesta after lunch; even half an hour will help restore your flagging energy. Don't stay up late just for the sake of it. If there is a dance or something to stay up for then, by all means, continue till dawn, if you are enjoying yourself. I think the secret of not being tired is to drink very little after you have had your cocktails and wine at dinner, because if you go on drinking, you get sleepy and long for bed. When I was a young man I hardly drank at all. I would go the round of night-clubs in Paris, London or New York, drinking Vichy water with a slice of lemon. It was the Merchant Navy that taught me the pleasure of drink.

If your mother wanted you to be born a girl and you were born a boy, what would you do? Try again and

The present Earl and Countess of Pembroke on their wedding day, 1989 (*photograph: Henry Wills*)

hope the next child would be a girl? Not Lady Glenconner. She decided to treat her son Stephen as a girl.
He was dressed in female clothes until he reached the
age of ten and then put into clothes resembling Little
Lord Fauntleroy, with ringlets down to his shoulders.
No wonder he grew up to be the extraordinary
Stephen Tennant. He was incredibly good-looking and
very vain. He would spend hours in front of the
looking-glass, trying different shades of rouge, lipstick
and the rest. One day he asked my father, whom he
called 'Cousin Reggie' (although he was no relation),
if he could borrow the estate lorry to drive him to
Grovelly Wood to dig up some peat for his azaleas, as
the garden soil at Wilsford was chalk. My father said:
'Of course, Stephen old boy'. Now, the driver Bennet
was an extremely handsome young man. Later, in his
Wiltshire accent, he told me that when they got to the
wood, it happened to be bluebell time. Stephen said to
him: 'Oh, Bennet, let's lie down amongst the
bluebells.' 'I put down my spade and did as I was told.
Then Mr Stephen held my hand.'
'What did you do?' I asked.
I said: 'You are a very nice gentleman, Mr Stephen,
but I have never been unfaithful to Mrs Bennet and I
am not going to start now!'
On another occasion Stephen telephoned his
brother, Lord Glenconner, who, as head of the family,
controlled their finances, to ask if he could move his
house, Wilsford, stone by stone, to a location by the
sea. Christopher explained that it would be quite impossible and far too expensive. Stephen was crest-
fallen, but only for a short time. About six months
later he rang me up and said: 'David, come and have
lunch with me by the seaside.'
'Where?' I asked.

'Here, of course.'

I thought, this time Stephen really has gone nuts.

I arrived at one o'clock to find Stephen, in a bathing-suit, sitting in a deck-chair on what was once the lawn. Sweeping down to the river was truckload after truckload of sand, which he had imported, entirely obliterating the lawn. On the other side of the river he had painted an enormous background of sea, on which ships were sailing happily on the waves, dolphins popping their heads above the water and jumping fish. These aquatic touches, together with life-size figures of men and women cut out of cardboard sunbathing in the near-nude, completed the panorama. It is rather wonderful to be able to go ahead with your original idea by turning it into a make-believe world. It is a form of optimism – refusing to be thwarted and never taking no for an answer.

# 6

Elsie de Wolfe, later Lady Mendl, decided that when she died she should be placed in a large cannon and shot out over her beloved Versailles, where she had lived for many years. But when the time came, as she was dying, she regained consciousness for a second or two. Her last words were: 'They can't do this to me!'

Sir Charles married Elsie late in life. This was a white marriage and suited both of them, as he was an impecunious bachelor with a title and she was very rich. Harold Nicolson told me that when he and Charles were young men, both working at the British Embassy in Paris, they shared an apartment and that every morning while Charles was shaving, looking at himself in the mirror, he would say over and over again: 'I am handsome, I am rich and I am a Christian!' I don't know why he minded being Jewish, as there have been so many successful Christian Jewish marriages in the British aristocracy – Lady Louis Mountbatten was the granddaughter of Sir Ernest Cassel, Sybil Sassoon married the Marquess of Cholmondeley, Venetia Stanley married Edwin Montagu and Lady Peggy Primrose, daughter of the Earl of Rosebery, married the Marquess of Crewe, to name but a few. Edward VII was surrounded by Jewish friends. The Samuel family were ennobled, taking the title of Baron and then Viscount Bearsted. Rufus Isaacs became Marquess of Reading, and then of course there are the Rothschilds, but they are different, a law unto themselves.

In my young days, when living in New York, I had the privilege of knowing the Gershwins, the Kaufmans, Ethel Merman, Alexander Woollcott – in fact most of the intelligentsia of that period. But I suppose that Dorothy Parker was the wittiest and most fascinating of them all. I remember going down to a beautiful house in Maryland with Noël Coward, Dorothy Parker and Gladys Calthrop. This house had been bought by some *nouveau riche* New Yorker. We approached it by a splendid avenue of trees, all about sixty feet high. Our host was on the doorstep to greet us. Noël said: 'I've seldom seen such a wonderful avenue anywhere in the world.' The owner replied: 'When we bought it, only one side of the avenue remained, so we bought and transplanted the other side with trees exactly the same height as the original ones.' Dorothy Parker said quietly: 'Marvellous. It makes one think what God could have done if he'd had money!' I think it was she who made of Tallulah Bankhead, who had appeared in a play called *Cleopatra*, a one-line criticism: 'Miss Bankhead sailed down the Nile last night and sank.'

In the 1930s Cecil Beaton had an apartment in the Waldorf Astoria Hotel in New York. So did I. Cecil was at the height of his fame as a photographer but, not satisfied with this accomplishment, he started to draw seriously. Also staying in the hotel was Gloria Swanson and her handsome husband Michael Fermer. One day Cecil asked Gloria if she would mind her husband posing in the nude. 'Of course, darling. Michael, I'm sure, will be highly flattered. How long will it take?' 'Only an hour or so,' said Cecil. Well, it took a great deal longer. Gloria was getting restless and, rather than interrupt the artist at his work, she sent a bellboy with a scroll of paper tied by a pink ribbon. Cecil opened it. Inside was a drawing of a male organ with the words: 'Darling, I think it's time I had him back, if you don't mind. Love, Gloria.'

Another well-known actress had just been left by her husband for another woman. She got paralytically drunk and fell into bed pretty well unconscious. She was woken by a hand feeling all over her body, and suddenly the voice of the wandering hand exclaimed: 'Whaat, no cock?'

In Paris during the 1940s when Diana and Duff Cooper were British ambassador and ambassadress, they entertained in a lavish way. People of all nationalities and from all walks of life would attend their poetical parties in the Salon Vert. Bébé Berard, the painter, seldom moved without his little dog. It was not housetrained and was always making messes on the Aubusson carpet. Diana eventually said to him: 'Really, Bébé, this carpet belongs to the government, not to us. So if you must bring your dog, please keep it in your arms.' One evening Bébé forgetfully put his dog on the floor, where it immediately made a large mess. Bébé quickly looked around, grabbed the turd and put it in his beard. True love can go no further.

Another extraordinary hostess was Marie-Louise Bousquet. She had very little money, but once a week she held a soirée in her small apartment in the place du Palais Royal. There was nothing to eat and practically nothing to drink, but the company was so stimulating and Marie Louise such a strong character that her apartment was always full to overflowing. This is a good example of money not always counting. You can go to some rich people's parties where caviare and foie gras are piled in heaps, and where champagne flows, yet you are bored to death.

Joan Clarkson was an amusing, beautiful and witty

Patricia, Dowager Viscountess Hambleden, the author's
sister

woman. She was one of C.B. Cochran's (the great impresario of British musical comedies and revues in the 1930s) 'Young Ladies', as they were called. They were lovely to look at and Joan was the loveliest of them all. Years later at a party given by Noël Coward, Noel said: 'Now we will play a new game. Everyone, in turn, must make up a rhyme about themselves. Joan, you first.' In a flash Joan said: 'I was once a beautiful English rose, a rose that Mr Cochran chose, but now that I've flopped and my petals have dropped, they'll make a pot-pourri of me.' 'Game over,' said Noël. 'No one can beat that!'

Graham Payne, one of Noël Coward's protégés and best friend who danced and sang in many of his operettas and revues, once told me of an incident that took place when Noël lived in the West Indies. One morning, Noël was busy in the kitchen preparing lunch when there was a knock on the door. It was very hot and he was wearing only an apron. The caller was the local clergyman come to pay his respects. Noël said: 'Just a minute while I turn off the gas.' When he returned, the clergyman had fled. Noël had forgotten that he was only wearing an apron and, on turning round, had unwittingly displayed his bare behind.


I would suggest that you make a point of learning at least two foreign languages. It will make your life a great deal more interesting, either if you want a job or if you travel abroad for pleasure. French and Spanish are the two most important, as they cover most of South America and a large part of Europe. Don't be shy about making mistakes, as foreigners enjoy that and will help you out if you get stuck. Writing this reminds me of a series of funny mistakes, told to me by my father, about an extraordinary American lady called Mrs Moore. This happened about 1903. She spoke terrible French but refused to talk her own language. She lived high up in the Alpes-Maritimes, where in winter it quite often snows. My parents arrived that winter to stay with her. It was snowing and pinned to the front door was a message which read: *Pendant l'hiver, entres par mon derrière.*

Two other stories that are worth telling were told to me by my father and by my mother respectively. They were staying in the same hotel as Mrs Moore. My father met her one morning and said: 'How are you today? I hope you had a good night.'

'Non,' she replied. 'J'ai couche sur un sal matelot.'

My mother was driving with her in a horse-drawn carriage along the Croisette in Cannes. Mrs Moore wished to let down the little seat in front of her on which she wanted to rest her feet. She couldn't manage it and shouted to the coachman: 'Cocher, cocher, montrez moi votre petit chose qui peud devant.'

These mistakes caused much amusement and were quoted at dinner parties all over France. So you see, mistakes can be a help rather than a hindrance.

I am not interested in sport. In a way I am fortunate, because people who have a passion for it find, after the age of say sixty, that physically they can't cope with strenuous exercise and so have to give up golf, tennis, riding and most outdoor sports. They rely on television for sporting events. Also they age quicker than indolent people, because their muscles turn to fat, so they become flabby – football players suffer the most, golf players the least.

I am not really a card player either, though I do play cards from time to time. I am certainly not a gambler either; playing cards should be for fun. Of course it is more exciting to play for small stakes rather than none, but if you play for high stakes it often ends in squabbles and recriminations if you or your partner are bad losers. I refused to learn bridge for that reason. As a boy I was horrified at how disgracefully the grown-ups behaved, each blaming the other if they lost a rubber, some even leaving the table and refusing to continue when they didn't win. Games like poker, roulette and so forth are another matter, for it is just a question of luck, so you can blame no one.

If you grow up to be an inveterate gambler, nothing will stop you. But if you realize you are a bad loser, don't play games in which you have a partner, for it can very easily destroy friendships.

Lady Baillie was a great gambler and very rich. The joke going round Monte Carlo was that they knew when Olive had lost, because she left the casino wreathed in smiles. When she won, she left with a miserable expression on her lovely face – she couldn't get rid of her money quick enough!

If you are interested in clothes and want a career as a couturier, the first thing to remember is to design classic rather than attempt to be fashionable by designing executive clothes. The latter may have a success for a while, until your clients realize that they can't wear this or that dress more than once or twice. People will say: 'Not that get-up again'. If you stick to the classic and not too showy kind of dress, you can wear it again and again. The really great couturiers such as Chanel, Lanvin, Dior and particularly Molyneux are the four that come to my mind, for they never date. I recall in the thirties the Marchioness Curzon of Kedleston gave a coming-out dance for her granddaughter. Grace Curzon was a great beauty, as was her daughter Marcella. Her granddaughter was also a very pretty girl. Grace decided that it would be an amusing idea that all three of them should wear dresses designed by Edward Molyneux, an old friend of hers. She herself wore one made for her many years before. Marcella was told to wear the dress that she had worn at her coming-out dance some twenty years earlier, and Edward designed a new creation for the granddaughter. All three looked the height of elegance in dresses spanning a good seventy years.

Don't be a grumbler, forever complaining about things. It's tiresome and inexcusable, as all you have to do is look around and see the misery of some people's lives in comparison with your own. When sometimes I do complain to myself, I at once say: 'Shut up. How dare you!' It works and I snap out of it. I think that most grumblers lack friends, as no one wants to listen to their endless hard-luck stories, which in reality, most likely, don't even exist except in their imagination. Grumbling is a mixture of stupidity and egoism, and stems from having nothing of interest to say.

Try not to show that you are worried about something. Your friends will notice any anxiety you reveal straight away and start asking you what's the matter. This will be embarrassing, because nine times out of ten it is a personal worry which you don't want to share with anyone. They mean well, in attempting to help you through whatever it is that is troubling you, but in reality they will only make things worse and you will find yourself concocting some ridiculous excuse, which won't fool them for one moment. Then their curiosity will become so intense that they will bang on asking you questions until you give in and pour out your troubles, which will be immediately discussed with other friends until they become the talk of the town! Hide your worries, keep a stiff upper lip and keep on smiling pleasantly if you can.

It is interesting to see how one behaves in a traumatic situation, such as being torpedoed, as I was during the Second World War when I was wireless operator on the troopship *Strathallan*. The first reaction was one of shock and then a moment of panic ensued. Suddenly a different side of my character took over and I remember saying to myself 'Pull yourself together, David', after which I became calm and I hope fairly efficient. There were so many things to do and so many people to encourage that I had no time to think of the danger I was in. I suppose the good Lord gave me a sort of protective covering which in a strange way stifled my imagination so that I stopped thinking of what might happen if the worst came to the worst. So many of the soldiers, American and British, were very young and for them it was a terrible experience, as they had never been close to danger before. Some took it in their stride; others were frankly terrified, and it was pathetic to see them trying to be brave. My heart bled for them.

I am not squeamish and rarely upset by unpleasant happenings, but one incident comes to my mind which really horrified me almost to death. After I was torpedoed I joined a very hush-hush organization called DDODI, involved with collecting tired spies from France and replacing them with fresh ones. These operations were carried out in small, high-powered ships disguised as French fishing-boats. A young American was sent to join the flotilla based in the Helford river to learn about our goings-on. He was charming and good-natured but a bit too sure of himself and he would never listen to advice. He was warned about the strong currents and not to swim at

The writer Paul Bowles on the cliffs near Tetuan
(*photograph: Phillip Ramey*)

certain times in certain places. He ignored this warning and one day went missing. The river was dredged as far as the open sea and at last his body was found. As it came to the surface we could see that the entire body was encrusted with lobsters. It was a truly gruesome sight and it took me many years before I could even look at a lobster, let alone eat one.

To be courageous, I don't mean physical courage but to bear horrifying experiences with calm and dignity, is a noble trait. I am lucky to have such a friend. She is Sheikha Fatima al-Sabah, sister-in-law to the future Emir of Kuwait. Two of her brothers were captured by Saddam Hussein during the Gulf War and maltreated as only that monster could maltreat people. Fatima remained here surrounded by nephews and nieces who, thank God, had escaped. She had no news of her brothers and told me later that she thought she would never see either of them again. She seldom went out and spent her time cherishing all these fatherless children, who were forever asking about their fathers. It takes real courage to appear confident and not break down under the strain of those many months. The relief that it is all over must be overwhelming, but I feel it will take some time before she is her dear, charming self once more.

## 7

I suppose I was rather in love, as a boy of ten, with my sister's French governess, Mademoiselle Ferré. She wore large straw hats, winter and summer, with blue satin bows and bunches of flowers round the crown. She appeared to me to be the acme of romance! During the same period my mother had a secretary called Miss Belmont. She was pretty in a faded way but seemed to suffer permanently from a cold in the head. Mademoiselle Ferré had complete power over her and would take her for long walks through the woods at night to a little pavilion designed by Chambers in the eighteenth century called Temple Copse. What went on there I have no idea, but suddenly Miss Belmont left and Mademoiselle Ferré went quite mad and was found by my startled mother lying outside her bedroom door proclaiming everlasting love. She was never mentioned again, but I often wonder what happened to her. I fear she was removed to an asylum of some sort in France.

It seems that my mother, who was very beautiful, was fascinating to this type of lady. Another secretary once said to me: 'I think your mother is the loveliest human being I have ever seen. I would like to run my fingers over every feature of her perfect face.' I said: 'I shouldn't do that if I were you or you will be out on your ear in no time!' I'm sure this particular lady was totally innocent but just hypnotized by beauty.

When my mother left Wilton after the death of my father she moved to a stone house called Lambridge, near Henley-on-Thames. Here she had a series of couples to look after her, but like so many older ladies, she conceived a sort of passion for a man-of-all-work called Mr Bud. He could do no wrong, rather like Queen Victoria and John Brown. I couldn't bear him and I am sure he made a packet of money out of her. Fortunately, she later moved to London where Bud couldn't get at her any more.

People imagine, that if you are brought up, as I was, in a wonderful house like Wilton, that you automatically have good taste. This is far from the truth. My grandmother disliked Wilton and referred to it as a horrid, damp place. When my grandfather died she moved to a remarkably ugly house called East Knoyle. It was not far from Wilton but on much higher ground and she and my Uncle Geordie, her second son, lived happily in this monstrosity until she and Uncle Geordie died. My father had no taste either, nor had my younger brother Tony. I think taste comes from vision, so if you can't see beauty, how can you have taste?

I love my possessions with a passion. Being a second son I had to start from scratch, collecting things from antique shops all over the country. I realize now that I must have been born with taste, as the pictures, furniture, and so on that I bought then for a pittance are three or four times more valuable today. It is a real comfort to me to be surrounded by the objects I love, and each one reminds me of times in days gone by.

Another aspect of taste that I find interesting is the case of women's clothes. Some of the best-dressed women I have known have absolutely no taste whatsoever in doing up a house and are forced to employ an interior decorator. Whereas some of the worst-dressed women have perfect taste in decorating their houses.

One day long ago the late Lady Salisbury and I

were leaving a luncheon party given by Muriel Ward in her house in Hampstead called Cannons Lodge. I said to Betty Salisbury: 'What is it about that house that makes it so individual, warm and attractive?' She replied: 'Pre-taste, darling!'

I was a hopeless student and unable to pass exams, even though I knew the answers perfectly. The moment I sat down to take an exam, my mind became a total blank. In all the four years I was at Eton, I never once passed end-of-term exams, which meant I had to return there two days earlier at the end of the holidays to try again. I was lucky in that I had a sympathetic housemaster called Samuel Gurney Lubbock, who was married to the famous pianist Irene Scharrer, second in fame to Dame Myra Hess. She was seldom at home, owing to the fact that she gave concerts all over the world. She and her husband had two heavenly young children, Ian and Rachel, whom I loved, and I think they loved me. When their mother returned on fleeting visits, there was an upheaval in the household and the nannies all left. Mr Lubbock would send for me to play with the children and sometimes even bath them and put them to bed. For this reason I was not superannuated for failing in my exams. Rachel became a very good actress, and I believe she is still alive and well. Ian, who also went on the stage, is I think dead. They were an enchanting family and helped to make my school life very happy, though I was naughty and broke every possible rule, for which I was soundly punished by being given a good beating by the headmaster!

Mr Lubbock was a bit of a dreamer. He rarely had meals with us but when he did the food was quite good. However, when he was absent, it was nearly uneatable – organized by a woman called Miss George. Each house had one of these supervisory ladies and they were referred to as 'the Dame'. The meals usually consisted of cod with egg sauce, or boiled beef and cabbage with old string beans and potatoes with black heads in them, followed by dry rice pudding or some revolting wobbly jelly. We struggled to get it down and then, when we were free, rushed to the tuck-shop in the town and stoked up with goodies which we smuggled into our rooms and hid under our mattresses. I am told that today the food is excellent and the boys have no reason to complain.

When I was in my late teens England seemed full of eccentric ladies and gentlemen. I have already written about several of them, but I have suddenly remembered Wenefryde Greaves. Born Tollemache and married to a delightful man nicknamed the 'Gredbe', she and her husband lived modestly in a small house close to my cousin Michael Duff's house Vaynol on the Menai Straits, near Bangor. Wenefryde had a statuesque figure and was always bubbling with humour. She woke up one morning to find she had inherited Ham House, a castle in Scotland and a huge country house in the Midlands, added to which she became Countess of Dysart in her own right. Quite an inheritance! The jewellery which went with all this wealth was fabulous. Quite soon after this happened (they had still not moved from the little North Wales house), Michael gave a ball. When the dance was in full swing Wenefryde entered, wearing an enormous tiara and all the jewellery she could pin on. She sailed up to Michael, who started to say 'My dear, how wonderful . . .' when Wenefryde said: 'I will just drift round the room for a minute or two – as a kind of rehearsal for what my future life will be since my inheritance – and then go home. I always believe in leaving on the crest of a wave!'

The author with Barbara Hutton at a party at her house in Tangier

Later when she was ensconced in all three houses, she asked me to go and stay in the Scottish castle. I said: 'Wenefryde, I never seem to go to Scotland, as I don't shoot or stalk or fish – anyway, I hate killing animals.' She replied: 'Come just the same, and we will kill each other with kindness.'

Having kicked around the world when I was young and having spent four years in the Merchant Navy I have come in contact with every kind of person you could imagine. This was a godsend, as I find it easy to adapt myself to any circumstance or any individual, however different they are from me. Hence, life flows through my meeting new acquaintances. Some become friends, some drift out of my life, but each encounter is fascinating and makes life fuller and richer. I suppose it means I am a complete extrovert and give all I can to whomever I am with who will bother to listen to me!

A quirk in some people's character is the enjoyment they get out of shocking someone who is really upset by use of filthy language or dirty stories. It is a form of sadism to enjoy watching faces crumple with distaste or blush from embarrassment. And it is pointless and unkind. I am unshockable but frequently offended by this sort of behaviour. The best way to cope with such people is calmly to remove yourself from their presence with a show of complete indifference.

Mockery is an unattractive trait, the perpetrator always belittling things that don't happen to amuse him, such as village fêtes, bazaars, Girl Guides, rallies, Boy Scouts and so on. These things are an integral part of life in every country. To enjoy outings you must join in the fun and often, if you are not over-sophisticated, you can have a jolly good time.

Don't be afraid to speak your mind if you feel it is

the only way to get something done, such as help save some architectural gem – an old stable, for instance, which is falling down and which, with a few thousand pounds, could be repaired; or a folly in park of some old estate now turned into a school or a boat-house designed by William Beckford. Alvilde Lees-Milne is an adept at this and will go for the owners of these past glories hammer and tongs, denouncing them to their faces as Philistines. By her outspokenness she has managed to save many buildings of historical interest. How she has time and the energy past the age of eighty to do so many things, is a mystery to me. Apart from what I have just written, she is designing and working on three gardens – Giscard d'Estaing's garden in France, King Hussein of Jordan's near Ascot, Mick Jagger's, also in France, and recently Mick Jagger has bought a house in Richmond, where she is also designing the garden. She stands no nonsense from the owners if they say: 'Are you sure that's a good idea?' She will reply: 'If you think my ideas aren't good, why employ me?' Her own garden in Essex House, Badminton, although small, is a dream of delight. She really is a genius where gardens are concerned and equals Vita Nicolson's (Sackville West's) garden at Sissinghurst or Nancy Lancaster's at Hasley in Oxfordshire. She is one of my closest friends and comes regularly to stay with me in Tangier. She is kind enough to say that my garden is OK.

Don't lose your temper if you can possibly help it. I rarely do, but when I do I always regret it. It usually happens if one is overtired or not feeling well and one's reflexes are not acting properly. If after an outburst you leave the room, the person on whom you have vented your wrath may say: 'What on earth made so-and-so lose his temper in that ridiculous way? After all, I only said, etc. etc. He must have had a liver attack or had one drink too many!' It is much more effective to keep your cool. If you really are angry, walk out of the room in silence. I know some people, on the other hand, who lose their temper on purpose just to create a scene and then listen quite peacefully to people squabbling together about some totally unimportant subject. I suppose it's their idea of fun. It's certainly not mine!

Lord Penrhyn of Penrhyn Castle in North Wales was always in a bad temper, cursing everyone around him whether they were servants or friends, but his delightful wife suffered the most. My cousin Michael Duff, who was his neighbour, said that sometimes he would stack up valuable plates and hurl them across the room, quite often hitting his wife in the face. Fortunately she had no children by him. At last she escaped and married again, a charming man, Lord Fortescue, by whom she had a son and lived happily in the Cotswolds till she died a few years ago. Lord Penrhyn never remarried and was succeeded by a niece. Penrhyn Castle is now in the hands of the National Trust.

Playing the part of being innocent was much in evidence when I was in my teens. The two real examples of this were the Countess of Beauchamp and the Countess of Shaftesbury, sisters of the far from innocent Duke of Westminster. I recall many amusing stories about them. Lady Shaftesbury was called Cuckoo (cousin Cuckoo to me) and she had three daughters and two sons. The eldest son, Tony, married Sylvia Hawkes, a beautiful courtesan, and was cut off by the family. They divorced and secondly Sylvia married Douglas Fairbanks Senior. The eldest daughter married Lord Allington and the second daughter, known as Dotty, married Ivor Churchill and afterwards Anthony Head.

Queen Mary, on Dotty's engagement, sent a message to Lady Shaftesbury asking which of her daughters was engaged, as she was godmother to one of them. Lady Shaftesbury replied: 'Dotty, Mam. Cuckoo.' One year we spent Christmas and New Year with them at St Giles, a lovely house, alas now falling to pieces, while our parents were on a cruise. Cousin Cuckoo went away for a few days, during which time her parrot, which she was supposed to love, died. Miss Harman, her secretary, didn't like to bury it until Cousin Cuckoo returned, so she placed it in a cardboard box in the vestry of their private chapel. On returning she asked where Polly was. Miss Harman nervously replied: 'Oh, she died and I placed her in the vestry.' 'Really, Miss Harman, not on the altar? What a shame!' She was very fond of me and had the extraordinary idea that I should become Bishop of Salisbury. 'David darling, you would make such a dear little bishop dressed in all those pretty clothes.'

The Duchess of Portland was another remarkable lady. Beautiful, unpredictable and slightly eccentric. She lived with the Duke in almost royal splendour at Welbeck Abbey in Nottinghamshire, surrounded by thousands of acres. Welbeck was vast and ugly but filled with wonderful pictures and furniture, including the famous Portland vase. At the beginning of the Second World War the Eagle Squadron, consisting of American flying officers who had volunteered to come over and help us before the United States entered the war, were stationed near Welbeck. Michael Duff was their liaison officer and told me that Winnie Portland asked him to bring them over for a tour of the Abbey. They trooped through room after room, the Duchess explaining each treasure. At last the tour came to an end in a smaller room, where she said: 'That's a Rembrandt, that's a Titian, that's a Rubens and, pointing to an armchair, that's Portland (where dozed the comatose Duke), that's a Raphael, that's a Van Dyck', and so on. The Americans were quite hysterical with laughter. Another story concerns a guest who was met at the station by a hired car. On the visitor's arrival at the Abbey, Winnie said: 'So sorry, my dear, but the first eleven footmen are playing cricket against the first eleven chauffeurs.' When in Paris she liked walking everywhere looking at the shops but, since she didn't have a very good bump of locality, she had a piece of cardboard pinned to the back of her coat which read *Si je suis perdue rendez moi au Ritz*.

Once when she arrived at Euston Station one of her footmen was not on the platform to meet her. She didn't know what to do. The porter suggested that she telephone her home, so she entered the telephone-box accompanied by him. The story goes that when the voice answered and said press button and put in 2 pennies please, she replied: 'Put it down to me. I'm the Duchess of Portland!'

When in London one would find her every morning sitting at the first table on the right as you entered the big dining-room of the Ritz Hotel, writing letters. As the restaurant started filling up, the head waiter would bow to her and ask what Her Grace would like for lunch. Continuing to write, she replied: 'More ink please!'

These stories may make her sound ridiculous but she was adored in Nottinghamshire and was a true lady bountiful, always interested in anything around her and helping the miners and their wives working in the coal-pits in this distressed area.

The author in his garden in Tangier

Lady Beauchamp was purportedly always 'in the clouds', but I really don't think she was in the least. Eddie Tatham and I thought it would be fun to ask her if we could row her round the moat at Madresfield Court, their lovely house near Malvern. When we got in the boat we surreptitiously dropped anchor but went on pretending to row. After about ten minutes we stopped and said: 'Wasn't that fun, Lady Beauchamp?' 'Delicious,' she said, with a seraphic smile. 'Not a ripple and so quick – usually it takes half an hour!' We felt very silly.

Another time, my father told me that she said to him: 'Reggie, dear, I don't understand why the King asked Will Will (her husband) to leave England' (there had been a scandal about his homosexual tendencies). 'Benny (Duke of Westminster) tells me it's because Will Will's a bugler.'

To be gracious without appearing condescending is difficult. Members of royal families are born and bred to it, so to them it is part of 'the job', but I am thinking of famous people such as ministers and presidents and their wives, movie stars and so forth. To my mind, one of the most outstanding examples of this characteristic was Eleanor Roosevelt. Very tall, rather ungainly and certainly no beauty, she had dignity and graciousness just by being herself. I met her once in my life and was so impressed that I still remember the occasion, which was during the Second World War in London when I was on leave. She was accompanied by Queen Elizabeth, the Queen Mother, who is the epitome of what I have just written about, and therefore it was all the more remarkable that Mrs Roosevelt could hold her own against such odds.

Queen Helen of Romania caught me out one day. She was very short-sighted and, unbeknown to me, had recently acquired contact lenses. I was walking down one side of Bond Street in a great hurry when I saw Queen Helen and her sister on the other side of the street. I was already late for an appointment and thought it does not matter if I don't greet her, as she won't see me. To my embarrassment I heard: 'Cooee, David. You thought I wouldn't see you, but you made a mistake. With my new contact lenses I can see perfectly. I was too vain to wear spectacles when driving to functions in Bucharest, but now with these wonderful new inventions, if they shoot at me I can always duck to avoid the bullet!' She was a delightful character and full of humour. I mentioned her in *Second Son*, where at a party given by Chips Channon at the time of Princess Elizabeth's engagement there were many queens at the dinner. When Chips announced dinner, the ex-Queen of Spain naturally went in first. There was a pause – no one knew which of the other queens should go next. Queen Helen said: 'I'm going next because I am the only Red Queen.' Romania was then in the hands of Russians. She returned to Romania and, by a miracle, she and King Michael escaped just in time. They had a code sentence in which occurred the word 'rabbits', she told me. Queen Helen was in Bucharest, King Michael at the country estate. One morning he rang her up to chat and, at the end of the conversation, he said: 'I had a shoot yesterday and killed a lot of rabbits.' She immediately left by car to join him and they boarded a plane to safety. She spent her long exile in Italy and made a charming house in Florence.

If you are unfortunate enough to be born stupid, you can remedy it if you have an intellectual mother. Juliet Duff was such a case. Her mother, Lady Ripon, my Great-Aunt Gladys, was a brilliant woman, added to which she possessed beauty and charm. A great lover of the arts, she brought Diaghilev over to London for the first time and the Russian ballet was performed at Covent Garden under her auspices. She told my grandmother, her sister-in-law, that she suffered with a very stupid daughter but that she would have her so well educated that no one would ever know it. In this she succeeded. Juliet fortunately had a retentive memory and a deep admiration of her mother and so copied her in every possible way. She grew up to be the friend of people like Hilaire Belloc, H.G. Wells, Willie Maugham, Evelyn Waugh and others. Bulbridge, her home at the gates of Wilton, was renowned for its intellectual weekends.

Aunt Gladys was also a great *amoureuse* and at one moment society decided that she had gone too far when she posted a letter to a friend of hers and addressed the envelope on purpose to a certain gentleman whose wife was a rival of her current lover. The couple never spoke to each other again. Fortunately Queen Alexandra was a great friend of hers, so when the scandal reached her ears, she sent for Aunt Gladys and drove her up and down Rotten Row in Hyde Park, where all society gathered each morning. The incident was forgotten.

Sidi Mohammed Menebhi – the Moroccan Minister of War – was one of her conquests. He was knighted by Edward VII. To this day the most beautiful carpet covers the huge room in the Menebhi palace in Tangier, made by the Wilton carpet factory and presented to him by Aunt Gladys, one assumes for services rendered!

Her sister, Lady Maud Parry, wife of Sir Hubert Parry, the musician, was completely different and very eccentric. She thought her left leg was Roman Catholic so kept it outside her blanket at night. She couldn't bear having her family to stay, so once told her chauffeur to drive some of them in reverse the four miles from the station to her house. She was also told by my grandfather (her brother) that she must call on her neighbours when she first moved to the house in the New Forest. She sent the chauffeur to scout out the land first to see which houses had no steps going into the front halls. She then had her tricycle strapped to the car. On arrival she got out of the car, mounted her tricycle, told the chauffeur to ring the bell and, when the door opened, peddled as fast as she could into the front hall. After this episode most of her neighbours refused to respond to the bell.

At the wedding of her grandson, David Plunket Greene, who was seven feet tall, to Babe Magustie, she excelled herself in the middle of the service by shouting (she was very deaf) to my father: 'Reggie, the girl must be mad. Everyone knows that giants can't!'

# 8

Do you have spells of reading? I do. It's odd, but sometimes I read for weeks on end and then suddenly I stop and don't look at a book for perhaps a month or six weeks. I don't know why, perhaps my poor brain is so stuffed full that it can't take any more. It is irritating if you live alone, as I do – what on earth can one do day after day, evening after evening, except listen to the radio or watch television? Two fairly worthless pastimes. To be a telly addict is such a waste of time. As for so called 'telly dinners', I think they are hell. What's happened to conversation? It isn't my idea of fun to sit silently chewing away with my eye glued to the screen. The meal passes in dead silence and, if one attempts to say a word, the others say 'Hush!' Conversation in the old days was an integral part of life, as was letter writing. Now few letters are written, owing to the telephone. You can say in five minutes what would take a good half-hour on paper. So the next generation will have no record of how we lived during the last half of this century. In the past, memoirs were full of letters, which make them so much more alive than the attempted memoirs of today, which are all hearsay. It's a pity, but nothing can be done about it.

Nothing is more fun than having a good gossip from time to time, but you must be careful with whom you gossip. So much mischief can be made by repeating some innocent bit of news. Just a little distortion by one person and, by the time it gets back to you, through three or four other people, you hardly recognize what you originally said. Beware especially of people who say promise me you won't repeat this and then repeat it themselves all over the town, causing petty and unnecessary squabbles. The reason for this, I think, is that they have nothing better to do. My dearest friend, Anna Mckew, and I have our morning gossip on the telephone, telling each other what's been happening in Tangier, just to keep in touch, not to make mischief, although sometimes Anna can't resist 'stirring the pot', but only for fun, as she is the kindest person and is always ready to help people in their troubles – not only people, but dogs, cats, birds and even rats (I suspect) benefit from her compassion.

A town like Tangier, where the European community is not very large, is bound to be a rather gossipy place, resembling E.F. Benson's *Mapp and Lucia* and the rest of his novels. The British are inclined to stick together, the French equally so. My French friends tell me that their community here is just as gossipy as our own. There are not many Spaniards left, though in the past they were very much in evidence. The stories that fly around are really extraordinary, frequently without a grain of truth, but it replaces boredom for people who have nothing to do.


I became friends with Paul and Jane Bowles many years ago. Cecil Beaton and I had been lent a house in Tangier called Villa Mektoub by Loel Guinness. Paul and Jane were staying at the Hotel El Fahar on the Old Mountain, as was Truman Capote, Jack Dunphy and Tennessee Williams. Suddenly Cecil was called to New York to do the décor and clothes for *My Fair Lady*, while Truman was told that his first book *Other Voices*,

*Other Rooms* was to be published. As I was left alone in the Villa Mektoub I invited Paul and Janie to stay. It was a happy time except that Janie developed German measles and had to remain in isolation. She asked me to go to the grain market and ask 'Sherifa', a Moorish woman to whom Janie was much attached, if she would come to the house and sleep on the floor of her bedroom during her illness. As a reward she would give her a radio. I returned with the answer: 'I will sleep on the floor during your illness, but only if you buy me a taxi and a chauffeur's uniform.'

We decided to motor back through Spain and France. We spent most of the trip putting the hood of my Jaguar up and then down, as Paul was either too hot or too cold. Eventually we arrived in Paris, where we stayed about a week. Our final destination was England. I sent a telegram to my housekeeper, Mrs Quinn, saying when we were arriving. We landed at Southampton and drove happily to Wilton, only to find my house in the Park hermetically sealed, shutters closed and no sign of life. Even my dog was absent. The telegram had never arrived. It was autumn and the weather cold and the house had been shut up for two months. I was in despair and drove round to where my cook/housekeeper lived. We returned and eventually settled in.

Paul, who is always happiest when things go wrong, was in his element and a great help to me, whereas Janie became sulky, cross and very unlike her usual self. Paul and I decided to put her in Coventry, by locking her in her bedroom till she apologized, which she did pretty quickly. We then enjoyed ourselves for a few days. After which Paul and Jane left for London to see Paul's literary agent.

The television film *Poor Little Rich Girl* has quite recently appeared in England. I have written about Farrah Fawcett playing the part of Barbara Hutton in my last book, *Engaging Eccentrics*. The film is truly nostalgic to me, as when made up and dressed as Barbara used to dress, Farrah resembled her to such a degree that it brought tears to my eyes. Poor Barbara – what a sad life she had. Too much money can be more disastrous than too little, because she never really knew who her true friends were. She was amazingly naïve, whether by birth or from a desire to believe in what she wished to. I shall never know. How she could go on marrying over and over again, searching for something she never found, is a mystery, for she was far from stupid, in fact she was highly intelligent, well read and even wrote a book of poems which she had privately printed. The answer to all this, I suspect, is that she was sexually cold and therefore didn't enjoy sex very much.

The only time I ever saw Barbara really happy was during the four years she spent with Lloyd Franklin, her young English lover. He was a kind, dear young man and truly loved her for herself. Barbara told me: 'I shall never marry Lloyd. He is too young and some day he will find a nice English girl and have children.' That is exactly what happened. He married Penny Ausley and had one son, who is my godson (now a young man). The tragedy was that Penny and Lloyd were killed in a motor accident between Rabat and Tangier when he was a baby and Penny was pregnant. They are buried in the cemetery of our English church of St Andrews here in Tangier. Barbara, I know, mourned him greatly, but by that time she had married Raymond Duan who, after his marriage, became

Prince Chimpansec! His elder brother remained Maurice Duan.

Barbara was a plump girl when I first met her. She had a beautiful face, but her figure was not her best feature. She was shy and embarrassed by the size of her breasts, which for a débutante were remarkably large and out of fashion at that time, as women would strap them as tight as possible with strong brassières to appear to have no breasts at all. She went on a strict diet, and I am sure she ruined her health by endless 'banting', as it was then called. Years later, when she was much older, she had her breasts lifted, and I remember one evening sitting with her and Ira Belline, the painter, to whom I dedicated my first book, *Second Son*, and Barbara lowered her dress to show us the miracle that had been achieved. I must say they were a really beautiful sight to behold – firm, tip-tilted and exactly the right size! She was like a child with a new toy – at last her dream had come true. Far from being a shocking display it was deeply touching and lovable, so unlike the Barbara that the rest of the world imagined her to be.

Once, Barbara told me how surprised she was when, one evening, she had invited Peter Mann the author to come and see her. She received him in her bedroom. She had been resting and was still lying in bed. She said to Peter 'Do sit down', pointing to the end of her bed. He said: 'I must tell you that I am homosexual.' Barbara said she was so taken aback that for a moment she was speechless. She then said to Peter: 'The world knows that. I certainly wouldn't have asked you to come and see me in bed if you had been heterosexual, but your assumption is so distasteful to me that the conversation that I hoped we would have had must be postponed till I am in full evening dress wearing a tiara. Good-night.' She was was furious Peter had treated her 'as if I were a tart'.

The story that she died penniless is not true. What is true is that Materson, her crooked lawyer, had robbed her of all her actual cash. However, Barbara had an iron box hidden under her bed which was full of valuables – jewels which she had managed to save. This was what her devoted friend and male nurse, Colin Frazer, told me. Now she was bedridden, she had no more decorative use for them. So, at the end of each month, they would select some ring, bracelet or necklace, pawn it and pay the hotel bill. This continued till she died. She never lost her sense of humour and they would laugh together – Barbara so pleased with herself that she had managed to outwit Materson. Colin also told me that the last person to visit her was Cary Grant, whom Barbara had always loved, saying he was the cheapest husband of them all. He hadn't taken one penny from her during their marriage.

She left her house in Tangier to Colin, but by the machinations of wicked people the will was considered invalid, owing to 'the balance of her mind being disturbed' – perfectly untrue. She, with all her money, didn't indulge herself in things that one may imagine rich people would want. She didn't own a yacht or have a private plane. She had one car, a Rolls-Royce, which went everywhere with her, driven by her faithful chauffeur, Charles, whereas one might have expected her to have a fleet of luxurious limousines. As a young woman she was a keen tennis player, again a contradiction – even in Paris one would meet her running down the long passage in the Ritz, tennis-racket in hand, dressed in shorts on the way to some club or other. I always think that was her bond with Baron von Cram, a professional player who was caught and tortured by Hitler – not because he was Jewish, since he was pure Aryan, but because he had homosexual tendencies. He and Barbara had been friends for years before she married him. This was a mistake on her part, thinking that she could cure him of these tendencies. The result was yet another divorce.

Barbara had all her faculties up to the last moment of her life. Her beloved house in the Kasbah has been sold to some people whom we never see. I believe they are Japanese with Canadian passports. It's sad that all the beauty and glamour created by Barbara has completely disappeared.


The European community in Tangier are very conscious of birthdays. In England when you are an adult they are passed by in general without much celebration, unless of course you are a great celebrity. I think probably the reason for making so much of birthdays is because we are so few living in a foreign land. It's a good reason for a kind of get-together, and we all seem like children again, wrapping up our presents and drinking each other's health, with many more birthdays to come! I shall be eighty-four on 3 October 1992 – a pretty good age! Each year Adolpho de Velasco gives a dinner party for me in his lovely old palace in the Kasbah. He invites all my friends, not only English, but friends of every nationality – Moroccan, Spanish, French, Italian and so on. Princess Lalla Fatima always attends and cuts the birthday cake with me by her side. I am deeply moved by the extent of friendship and kindness that is bestowed on me each year.

Adolpho's parties are unique; he has a genius for entertaining. The great patio, which has small rooms leading off it, has three tables, each seating ten people, decorated with exquisite flowers and lit by many candles. The food is delicious (he cooks a lot of it himself) and the drink copious. He also has a small orchestra and after dinner we dance till the small hours of the morning. It is an event I look forward to, but I never believe he will remember the date of my birthday. Yet somehow he always does. Not only does it give me such pleasure, but all the guests are enchanted by his generosity and kindness.

When you enter the old walled city by the beautiful Moorish arch you go back hundreds of years. That part of Tangier is unchanged, although the rest of the city is being steadily ruined. Any beautiful building is ruthlessly destroyed, every wonderful old tree mercilessly chopped down. For instance, the Grand Socco was a dream of delight, with wonderful old trees, under which the flower-sellers would sit, and next to them the basket-weavers, then the sellers of fruit – everything that the tourists come to Tangier to see. All this has been swept away, to be replaced by unpoetical buildings of cement, great empty concrete spaces used for nothing or else as car-parks. Nothing traditionally Moroccan is left for the disappointed tourist to gasp at with pleasure. It is particularly sad when you think what marvellous taste the Moroccan had in the old days. In Spain all the most beautiful things to visit are Moroccan built during their years of occupation, such as Granada, Córdoba, Seville and so on. What they are doing here is not my idea of progress, if that is what the municipality call it.


Edith Olivier said in her *Journals*, published in 1989, that she saw 'no future for David' – and I didn't either.

I never looked to the future and was devoid of ambition and saw the years ahead only as one long lifetime of fun. I think the 1939 war changed all that because, when I became a wireless operator in the Merchant Navy, I had to develop a sense of responsibility. After all, when I was on watch the lives of thousands of servicemen were virtually in my hands. If I had fallen asleep or read a book, so that I missed some urgent message, it would have been my fault if we had been torpedoed or dive-bombed. If I had not continued sending out SOS messages when our ship was torpedoed, we should not have been picked up by a destroyer while drifting in our lifeboats. Even then, we lost four hundred lives.

After the war I took life more seriously and eventually started to write. My two previous books, *Second Son* and *Engaging Eccentrics*, received good reviews and sold well. This has encouraged me, once more, to put pen to paper and attempt to help others with the personal philosophy I have developed during my long life. The secret of happiness is to open your arms to all, for there is some good in every individual. If you do this, you can never be bored. You learn the frailties of people and try to stir them up, making them laugh and instilling them with a certain optimism, which so many people lack. The pessimist is usually a very unhappy person who, when he wakes up in the morning, turns his face to the wall, unable to bear the thought of another day. For these unlucky people there is rarely a cure, unless something wonderful happens which changes their attitude to life.